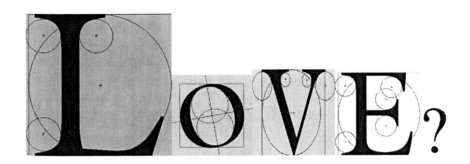

or

A GUIDE TO ACHIEVING PEACE AND HEALTH IN YOUR RELATIONSHIPS*
*meets the requirements of WAC 388-60 and RCW 26.50.150

Version 5.4

PARTICIPANT MANUAL

Doug Bartholomew MS, LMHC, Director,
Doug Bartholomew and Associates Inc.

iUniverse, Inc.
New York   Lincoln   Shanghai

Love? or Fear?
A Guide To Achieving Peace And Health In Your Relationships

Copyright © 2007 by Doug Bartholomew and Associates, Inc.

All rights reserved. No part of this book may be used or reproduced by any means, graphic, electronic, or mechanical, including photocopying, recording, taping or by any information storage retrieval system without the written permission of the publisher except in the case of brief quotations embodied in critical articles and reviews.

iUniverse books may be ordered through booksellers or by contacting:

iUniverse
2021 Pine Lake Road, Suite 100
Lincoln, NE 68512
www.iuniverse.com
1-800-Authors (1-800-288-4677)

Because of the dynamic nature of the Internet, any Web addresses or links contained in this book may have changed since publication and may no longer be valid.

The information, ideas, and suggestions in this book are not intended as a substitute for professional advice. Before following any suggestions contained in this book, you should consult your personal physician or mental health professional. Neither the author nor the publisher shall be liable or responsible for any loss or damage allegedly arising as a consequence of your use or application of any information or suggestions in this book.

ISBN: 978-0-595-47848-4 (pbk)
ISBN: 978-0-595-60043-4 (ebk)

Printed in the United States of America

"I didn't think that something so good could come from something so bad. We're getting along better now than before I was arrested, before the divorce. Actually, we're getting along better than we ever did even when we were married. She lives ten minutes from me, and our son comes and goes whenever he wants. I help her fix things around the house and help her with her car, and she helps me with family dinners. We had the holidays together. The other day we had a birthday party for my son and the whole family came over. He was so happy. He said he was glad Mom and Dad weren't fighting and said it was the happiest birthday he ever had. It was terrible that I assaulted her, and it was terrible that we got divorced, but in the end it stopped the abuse and made us a family–a different kind of family–but a family, for the first time."

—Marty, graduate of the program

CONTENTS

CHAPTER ONE: INTRODUCTION 1
    TO BEGIN WITH … 3
    THE ASSUMPTIONS 4
    BEFORE YOU START THE GROUP 10
    USING THIS BOOK 11
    WHAT HAPPENS IN GROUP? 13

CHAPTER TWO: ANGER MANAGEMENT 15
    WHAT IS ANGER? 17
    LESSON ONE: THE TIME OUT PLAN 21
    LESSON TWO: RATIONAL THINKING 24
    LESSON THREE: RELAXATION 31
    LESSON FOUR: CONFLICT MANAGEMENT 36
    LESSON FIVE: RELAPSE PREVENTION PLAN 43

CHAPTER THREE: DOMESTIC VIOLENCE 51
    LESSON SIX: WHAT IS VIOLENCE? WHAT IS VIOLATION? 53
    LESSONS SEVEN THROUGH NINETEEN: WHAT IS DOMESTIC VIOLENCE? 55
    LESSON EIGHTEEN: SOCIAL INSTITUTIONS WHICH SUPPORT CONTROL, ABUSE, AND VIOLENCE 102

CHAPTER FOUR: LEGAL ASPECTS OF FAMILY VIOLENCE 111
    LESSON TWENTY: LEGAL AND OTHER CONSEQUENCES OF DOMESTIC VIOLENCE 113
    LESSON TWENTY ONE: COURT ORDERS PERTAINING TO DOMESTIC VIOLENCE 117

SECTION FOUR: THE INVENTORIES 119
    LESSON TWENTY TWO: WHAT ARE ALL THE FORMS OF ABUSE YOU HAVE USED AND WHAT ARE THE ALTERNATIVES YOU ARE COMMITTING TO USING IN THE FUTURE 121
    LESSON TWENTY THREE: DEALING WITH OUR INADEQUACIES 124
    LESSON TWENTY FOUR: BEING A SAFE PERSON 126
    LESSON TWENTY FIVE: THE RESPONSIBILITY LETTER 130
    LESSON TWENTY SIX: THE EMPATHY LETTER 139

CHAPTER ONE

INTRODUCTION

TO BEGIN WITH ...

To begin with, I need to explain what this book is all about, and, more than that, to explain the assumptions upon which this model is based.

I'd like to start by making it clear that this is not about making you feel bad. Many times people have experienced approaches to these issues which are punitive or which feel the problems of this sort occur because of a failure to feel bad enough about yourself. Nothing could be further from the truth.

This is about becoming a better person.

This is not to say that you aren't a good person, only that the sort of things which get people to this point, things like anger or violence or trying to control loved ones, are in the opposite direction from becoming a better person. This is about getting back on track and having more meaningful, more peaceful relationships and becoming a better person.

It will make more sense if you read the following description of the assumptions upon which this approach is based. I'd like to encourage you to read them slowly so that you understand what we are hoping to achieve here.

To the degree that you agree with these assumptions, you will find it easier to understand what this is about, what is expected of you, and you will find it easier to succeed at our goals. Actually, I feel very strongly that these ideas are pretty acceptable to most of us, if not nearly everyone. I hope that they are to you, as well. They apply not only to the field of anger and violence and control, but also, I believe, to everything we do, in all parts of our lives.

The following three sections are broken down into single, logical steps. Each one lays the groundwork for the next one. They make the most sense if you read them in the order in which they are written.

As you read them, please stop at the end of each assumption and take the time to think about it and see if you agree with it, and, if not, why not. It works better if you think about each part as you go. That way, everything else in the book will make more sense and be easier for you to understand, succeed at, and apply to your life.

THE ASSUMPTIONS

PART ONE; HAPPINESS

1.
Happiness is our birthright. We have a right to be happy.
We don't have to explain, excuse, justify, apologize for, or feel guilty for being happy. It's our birthright.

2.
Happiness is natural.
We don't have to do anything to be happy.
If we aren't happy, it is due to an error of thinking or behavior.
If we correct the error, we will be happy.

3.
We are born knowing how to be happy.
We forget how later on.
Learning how to be happy is an act of remembering.
Whether we remember it in the blink of an eye, or over the course of a lifetime, we have to practice it every minute of every day in order to become proficient at it.

4.
Happiness is the only goal of life which makes sense.
Everything else in life is just a means toward that end, an objective toward that goal.

5.
Unhappiness occurs when we confuse the means with the end, which is happiness. This confusion is an error of thinking. If we correct this error of thinking, we can be happy.

6.
Seeking happiness from a false source, such as selfishness, materialism, power over other people, irresponsible sexuality, or other addictive, compulsive behaviors, is an error of thinking. Those things cannot possibly create happiness. It will inevitably fail.
If we correct this error of thinking and behavior, we will be happy.

7.
Blaming a false source for its inability to create happiness is an error of thinking and behavior, because those things cannot possibly create happiness.
It will lead to resentment, then anger, and ultimately violence to blame your unhappiness on something that can't possibly create happiness.
It is a sign that we have not learned the art of happiness.
Correcting this error of thinking will lead to peace and happiness. Failing to do so means that you are surrendering your life to failure, anger, resentment and violence.

8.
Happiness is not the absence of suffering.
There is inevitably a certain amount of suffering in life.
Struggling against this reality is an error of thinking and behavior which will leave you unhappy.
Correcting this error of thinking and behavior by accepting the reality of a degree of suffering in life will lead to happiness.

9.
Blaming other people or circumstances for our lack of happiness is a sign that we have not learned the art of happiness.
It is not the fault of other people or circumstances that we have failed to learn the art of happiness. When we correct this error of thinking we can become happy.

10.
Unnecessary suffering, strife, anger, and violence are the result of blaming others or the universe for the failure of our expectations.
The road out of unnecessary suffering and strife, anger and violence is to correct our erroneous expectations, our personal errors of thinking and behavior, not to change others.
The road out is to take responsibility for our own happiness.

PART TWO; REALITY

1.
We live in a cause and effect universe.
Everything is the result of everything which preceded it.

2.
We live in an orderly, lawful universe.
We may not know what the laws are, but everything which happens, happens lawfully.
The same laws which govern the behavior of atoms and molecules govern the behavior of galaxies and clocks.
The same laws which create rocks also create babies and symphonies.

3.
The universe is neither benign nor malignant.
It has no intentions.
Nothing is personal.
The same rain which helps the farmer hinders the hiker.
The same laws of chance which allow one person to win allow others to lose.

4.
We humans are a part of that lawful universe.
We are not exempt from the lawful universe.
Even though we may not know all the laws of human behavior, our behavior, and the responses other people have to us, are lawful.

5.
Although we are lawful parts of the universe, we are not passive parts of the universe.
Feeling helpless or victimized is an error of thinking, which can lead to ineffectiveness and unhappiness.
When we correct that error of thinking we can become effective and happy.

6.
We have no control over what is presented to us.
We only have control over how we respond to what is presented to us.
We create our lives by the responses we make to what is presented to us.

7.
Our beliefs create our perceptions.
Our perceptions create our thoughts.
Our thoughts create our actions.
Our actions create results.
Our results create our worlds and our lives.
Thus each of us creates our lives with our beliefs, our perceptions and our thoughts.

8.
If we have created an unhappy world through incorrect thoughts and actions, then we can create a happy world by correcting those thoughts and actions.

9.

If we work in harmony with the cause and effect laws of the universe we will have more peaceful, effective, successful lives, even when we don't get everything we want.

If we resist the laws of the universe and feel put upon by those laws and realities, we will surrender our lives to chaos, failure, and violence.

PART THREE; RELATIONSHIP

1.
Relationship is the most difficult art there is.
It requires mastery of all the other arts and skill sets there are for us to master.

2.
Relationship is the ultimate test of our ability to know who we are and to see the other person as they truly are.

3.
Relationship is not the goal.
Relationship is the process by which we learn.
We do not attain relationship.
We do relationship.

4.
Relationship is never about the other person.
The other person is necessary for us to practice our art of relationship.
If a relationship flourishes, it is a sign that we have good skill.
If a relationship founders, then we have more to learn.
It is not about the other person.
They are not responsible for our level of skill.

5.
Blaming the other person for the foundering of a relationship is an error of thinking and behavior.
It makes no sense.
It is like a painter blaming their canvas, or a musician blaming the audience.
If we correct this error of thinking and behavior, we will become more skilled at the art of relationship.

6.
All relationship is with ourselves.
We seek in the other person what we seek in ourselves.
We admire in the other person that which we would like to admire in ourselves.
We hate that in the other person that which we hate in ourselves.

7.
All love is self love.
All hate is self hate.
All anger is anger at ourselves.
All loathing is self loathing.
All acceptance is self acceptance.

8.

To learn to accept others, we must learn to accept ourselves.
To learn to love others, we must learn how to love ourselves.
To learn how to forgive others, we must learn how to forgive ourselves.
To learn how to have compassion for others, we need to learn how to have compassion for ourselves.

9.
The foundering or flourishing of relationship is the foundering or flourishing of our relationship with ourselves.
If we correct our relationship with ourselves our relationships with the other person will flourish.
Expecting to solve our personal issues in relationship is an error of thinking, which will lead to unhappiness. If we correct this error of thinking, we can find happiness.

9.
When relationship is done well, we are all on our paths to discovering ourselves in the other person and in ourselves, and they in themselves.

10.
When relationship is done well, we do not need the other person to comply with our wishes or meet our expectations in order to do relationship well.
That is an error of thinking.
That is our own responsibility.
When we correct that error of thinking we will be able to do relationship better.

11.
When we do relationship well, the other person is free to become who they are without us feeling as though this is doing harm to us becoming who we are.
It is complementary; my independence brings us closer, and our closeness makes us free.

BEFORE YOU START THE GROUP

Thank you for taking the time to review the assumptions upon which this program is based. I hope this makes it clearer what the program is about and I hope that it makes it easier for you to accept these goals as what you hope to accomplish.

Now let's move on to talking about how to make the best use of this book and of the program.

This is probably a somewhat awkward time for you, perhaps not what you'd like to be doing right now. But I hope to be able to be part of making this a time of positive change for you in your life. Most graduates of the program report that their lives and relationships are less violent, more loving, more fulfilling and successful. Some even find happiness. I hope that you can be one of those people.

Change is an inevitable part of life. We do things, we learn from our experiences, we do things differently, get different results, and change. That is the process of life. For that to be a positive change we need to have good information, a good attitude, support, and opportunity. We hope to help with all of that.

This is about making the changes which give you control over your life, over yourself, instead of control over others. This is about accepting that we have control over our lives instead of feeling controlled by other people, circumstances or events. We all create our lives by what we do, and what we do is controlled by what we think. Other people don't create our lives for us.

Until we understand that we have created our lives, that we are responsible for how we respond to our lives, that we are *able* to *respond* to our lives and the people in our lives, until we accept our responsibility for controlling our own lives without controlling other people, without blaming other people or circumstances, we will be doomed to frustration, anger, and relationship problems. Because that simply doesn't work.

Taking responsibility is empowerment. It means taking effective control of our lives.

There is a surprising peacefulness to that thought. That when we accept that responsibility, that we are *able* to *respond*, without blame, we can begin to have better lives, better relationships. We can be better people (WAC 388-60-0245, (6) (7))[1].

This isn't a program about giving up anything. Not a thing. It's about gaining a lot. A lot of happiness, a lot of intimacy, a lot of control over ourselves and our lives. It's about having healthier, happier lives. It's a program about becoming a better person. It's about becoming a person who can have safe, happy, fulfilling relationships. It's a program about taking responsibility for our happiness in life, and the happiness of those with whom we choose to be in relationship. Learning that we are *able* to *respond* and create happiness and safety.

---

1   Because this book is written in Washington State, these references are to Washington State laws which govern domestic violence program in order to verify compliance with those laws.

USING THIS BOOK

This book is not intended to be a substitute for therapy. It should only be used as a part of a therapy program led by a therapist who is trained and experienced in this field. Some states certify family abuse counselors, so, if that is the case in your state, you should be with such a therapist. It is intended to work as a structured approach to letting go of the insanity of control, abuse, anger and violence in relationships and finding the sanity of peaceful, loving, supportive relationships.

The workbook is broken down into four parts.

The first is **ANGER MANAGEMENT** (WAC 388-60-0245 (8)). Anger is not the cause of control, abuse, or violence, but anger can make a bad situation worse, so learning to control our anger is an important first step. This consists of five techniques which are important skills for avoiding relapses while you go through the program to address more underlying issues. The lessons about these techniques are;
1. Time out (WAC 388-60-0245 (8), (11))
2. Rational thinking (WAC 388-60-0245 (1) (2))
3. Relaxation
4. Conflict management (WAC 388-60-0245 (8))
5. Relapse prevention (WAC 388-60-0245 (11))

Read this section as soon as you get the book. Fill out the Time Out Plan as the homework assignment for your first group.

After that, bring in one completed homework assignment per week, no more, no less. Read your assignment to the group to get their input, and the input of the group therapist, as part of your weekly check in and group discussion.

It is important that you bring in one assignment per week. This is so you think about it twice each week; once when you do the homework, once when you come to group, not just all at the end for "catch up". Consequently, if you miss a week, or the group thinks you need to make changes in your homework, don't double up the next week. Just keep bringing them in one at a time.

The second section is **DOMESTIC VIOLENCE** (WAC 388-60-0245 (3), (4), (4) (g)). Most domestic violence is done when we aren't angry, so controlling our anger is only the first step. In the following lessons you will learn about the various forms of domestic violence. In each lesson you will report on what you have done in each of the categories of domestic violence, the effects it had on the other person or people, what you should do differently, and the amends you owe for what you did.

The lessons and assignments about domestic violence are;
6. What is violence? What is violation?
7. Physical abuse (WAC 388-60-0245 (4) (a))*
8. Sexual abuse (WAC 388-60-0245 (4)(b))*
9. Gender abuse*
10. Emotional abuse (WAC 388-60-0245 (4))*

11. Verbal abuse (WAC 388-60-0245 (4) (b)*
12. Psychological abuse (WAC 388-60-0245 (4) (d) (e))
13. Use of minimization, denial and blame (WAC 388-60-0245 (6), (7))*
14. Use of coercion, threats, intimidation and fear (WAC 388-60-0245 (2) (f)*
15. Social abuse and isolation*
16. Using children (WAC 388-60-0245 (5)*
17. Financial abuse (WAC 388-60-0245 (4) (c), (10))*
18. Social institutions which support control, abuse and violence (WAC-388-60-0245 (1), (2))
19. Abuse using the legal system

The third section is **LEGAL ASPECTS OF FAMILY VIOLENCE**.
20. Definitions of domestic violence and legal consequences of domestic violence (WAC 388-60-0245 (9), (13)
21. Court orders pertaining to domestic violence. (WAC 388-60-0245 (13)

The fourth section is the **INVENTORY**. This consists of
22. A summary of all the forms of abuse or violence which you have used, and the non-abusive alternatives you will use in the future. (WAC 388-60-0245 (8), (11))
23. A summary of the inadequacies, which motivated you to use control, abuse or violence, and your commitment to changing those inadequacies in the future.
24. The traits of being a safe person, which you lack, and your commitment to developing those traits in the future.
25. A responsibility letter, written as if the victim(s) would read it, in which you accept responsibility for what you did and it's consequences, and make your amends. (WAC 388-60-0245 (11))
26. An empathy letter, written from the victim(s) perspective, to make sure you can really and truly see it through their eyes, and have empathy and compassion for them

It may sound like a lot, but just take it one week at a time, one lesson at a time, and it will make sense.

After you have completed all the lessons, one at a time, and completed the 26 weeks of group, you can go into the monthly individual sessions. During that time you will practice the skills and traits you identified in lessons 22, 23, and 24, and make the amends you identified in lessons 25 and 26.

Even more important, it will be a time for you to work with your therapist identifying the inadequacies and issues you have identified as relating to your anger, control, abuse, or violence. This is about becoming a better person, and what better way to do that than working on the things which are standing in our way?

WHAT HAPPENS IN GROUP?

Many people are uncomfortable with the idea of group because of ideas they have been given which are probably incorrect. Group, done this way, is actually not unpleasant, and many of the men find the process very rewarding. It is a chance to work together with other men working on the same problem, sharing similar experiences and struggles. At times we have to face unpleasant realities about ourselves, our actions, or our lives. At times we have to look very hard in the mirror. But this isn't going to be a process of being yelled at, insulted, or unnecessarily confronted. It's supposed to be a process of learning, and showing, respect for ourselves and others, a chance to learn, and experience, good relationship skills. You won't be exposed to violent or disruptive people; if anyone behaves like that they will be taken out of the program. In return, we expect politeness and thoughtfulness from you, as well.

In group there are four to eight participants. The groups last about an hour and a half, but sometimes they go a little longer.

When you come to group, there is a sign-in sheet for you to sign, as a record that you were there. There are also weekly check-ins for you to fill out so that you can make sure that your own thoughts and feelings and words are reflected in your file for that evening. In addition to your name and the date, the check-in-sheet consists of

1. Have you used any time-outs that week? If so, a brief description of the situations.
2. Have you been involved in any conflicts that week? If so, a brief description of how you handled them.
3. Any successes you want noted for the week.
4. Any negative events which happened that week and how you felt about them.
5. An empathy statement, something which you have learned, felt or done which shows that you have learned empathy for the other person in the event which led to your being in the program.

<u>What is empathy?</u>

Empathy is what happens when we feel the feelings of another person. When we realize what the world looks like through their eyes, and when we realize that their struggles in life are really not much different than the struggles we all feel and deal with in life.

This is a crucial part of the program. When we learn the art of empathy, even when we are unhappy with something someone has done, we won't act out in anger or in blame. We will have the same patience with them that we would hope for if we made a mistake.

Consequently, with each weekly check in, and in most exercises, you will be asked to take the time to come up with one new statement of empathy for the other person, even if you aren't around them anymore. Essentially, empathy is the opposite of anger, control, abuse or violence.

Once we are in group, each person takes a turn reporting on their weekly check-in and reading their homework assignment for the week to the group, and we all discuss it. Since each person starts their homework assignments–

one for each of the twenty six weeks of the group therapy part of the program—when they come in, that means that by the time you complete the twenty six weeks you will have not only done each of the assignments, you will have heard each of the exercises reported on and discussed many times and had many chances to discuss those issues with the other men.

The rest of the time is spent discussing the personal issues that have come up related to the issues which we are all struggling with. This is the group therapy part.

By the time you have completed the group therapy part of the program you will have a pretty good idea of your personal issues, and are ready to address them privately in the six months of monthly individual therapy.

There is a piece of advice that new members almost always get from the older members of group, which is the bottom line truth of this program or any other process of change; you get out of it what you put into it. There is no down side to this program or any other process of change or growth. The success you enjoy depends only on how much of your time, energy and feelings you are willing to "put on the table."

I hope that your experience here meets or exceeds your personal expectations.

CHAPTER TWO

ANGER MANAGEMENT

WHAT IS ANGER?

<u>Anger is a feeling</u>

Control, abuse, and violence are not caused by anger. Controlling anger isn't the same thing as controlling our violence. But it's an important place to start.

Anger is a natural, life saving feeling, which, like other feelings, such as hunger or thirst, helps us to stay alive.

Feelings serve four natural functions.

1) They alert us that we have an unmet need.
    a) Hunger lets us know we are low of food
    b) Thirst lets us know that we are low on water.
    c) Fear lets us know that we are in danger.
2) They help us identify specifically what that need is, and direct us to a way to meet that need.
    a) Hunger not only gets us to focus on food, but often it's toward a specific food or food group that we are missing, such as craving salt.
    b) Thirst motivates us to look for water or other liquids.
    c) Fear draws our attention to the specific source of danger.
3) Feelings energize us to do what it takes to meet those needs.
    a) Hunger or thirst gives us the energy and motivation to go out and get the food and water we need.
    b) Fear motivates us to have the energy, sometimes heroic energy, to address the danger through the fight-flight-freeze response.
        i) If we are able to flee the danger, we run or get away.
        ii) If we can't get away, and we are able to fight back, we attack the danger to defend ourselves: we fight back.
        iii) If we can't flee, and we can't fight, we "freeze" or withdraw, hoping to minimize the danger to ourselves.
4) When the need is met, the feeling goes away.
    a) When we are full, we stop eating.
    b) When our thirst has been satisfied, we stop drinking.
    c) When the danger is gone, we stop fighting.

<u>Anger is a secondary feeling</u>

The feelings mentioned above are "primary feelings"; they relate to a specific unmet need. Anger, on the other hand, is more general. It signals that a primary need is unmet.

- We can get so hungry that we become angry
- We can become so frustrated we become angry
- We can become so frightened that we become angry

In this sense, anger is like the "check engine" light on the dashboard of your car. It signals *that* something is wrong, but doesn't tell you exactly *what* is wrong. We have to learn to stop when we realize we are angry and make sure we know what we are angry about.

- Are we angry at the driver in front of us in traffic, or are we angry because our life is out of control and we are wasting years sitting on a freeway when we really should be living a simpler life?
- Are we angry because our child made the same mistake in math for the third time, or are we angry because we are hungry, not getting enough sleep, and feel like an inadequate parent?
- Are we angry at our spouse for saying we don't make enough money, or are we angry because we agree with them?

These are important questions to ask, because there is a tendency to be angry at whoever and whatever is in front of us when we become angry, and usually that person or thing isn't the actual source of the anger.

The goal of anger management is to stop the expression of the anger long enough to figure out what the underlying problem is, and then to focus our energy on the problem, not on the person.

Anger is a monkey's tail

There are specific physical and neurological structures which are designed to respond to physical threats and, as mentioned above, to destroy the threat, escape the threat, or withdraw from the threat.

These mechanisms are great for responding to physical threats, life-endangering threats. However, we are very seldom faced with actual attacks which would endanger our lives. More often, probably ten thousand times to one, when we respond with anger, we are responding to something which isn't actually life threatening. It could be emotionally or psychologically threatening, but not physically threatening.

Unfortunately, this leaves us responding to frustrating social events with the same mechanisms which were designed to protect us from charging lions and tigers. Being threatened by a job interview is different than being threatened by a life threatening physical attack. Yet our bodies want to respond the same way.

Imagine how a job interview would go if you leapt across the table and bit the interviewer? How would returning a defective television to the store go if you threw the clerk to the ground and choked them for asking for the receipt which you lost?

Consequently our mechanisms for dealing with anger are outdated, but we are stuck with them. In that sense they are an "atavism". An atavism is something that served a purpose once, but no longer does, such as the tiny hint of a monkey tail fetuses have at a point in their development, or the gills we have during one state of embryonic development.

They served a valid purpose at one time, but they don't anymore.

So, while anger, like defecating or breeding, is a natural feeling, it isn't always perfectly adapted to modern life, so we have to be careful when and how we use it. Learning how, when, and where to use it, is a part of growing up. Like learning the right time and place to defecate, eat or breed.

Anger is a process

Anger isn't just one thing. The word refers to a series of things that happen one at a time.

First, we have to **perceive** something as a threat	Then we have to **think** about it and conclude it is worth being afraid of	This creates the **feeling** of anger	Then we **act** angry.	Then other people **react to us** as being angry and can become frightened or angry back.

So when we talk about "anger" we need to be clear which we are talking about;

1. our **perception** of danger,
2. our angry **self talk**,
3. the **feeling** of anger,
4. **acting** angrily, or
5. **being perceived by** others as being angry.

The expressions of anger can be abusive

Have you ever been frightened by someone who was angry at you? Did you ever stop what you were doing because of your fear of their anger? Have you ever avoided making someone angry because you were afraid of their anger, or changed what you were doing to avoid making them angry?

If so, you were being controlled by their anger. Displays of anger can be a form of control. How did it feel to be controlled by your fear of someone's anger? Did it make you like them more? Trust them more?

Think about it. How does it feel that someone you love might be afraid of you? Is that what you want out of love? Is that the way you want you to be perceived by your loved ones? Is that how you want to be remembered when you die?

Anger that is expressed in violent or frightening displays is a form of emotional and verbal abuse. It is one method of abuse. And that might be how you are remembered when you die.

It is important to mention at this point that most forms of control, abuse, and violence occur when people are not angry. For example discrimination, sexism, racism, financial controls, and so forth are usually done when perfectly calm. Consequently, while controlling our anger is a good place to start, it is only just that: a good place to start. Once we control our anger we have to look deeper and discover the rest of the ways we have controlled, abused or hurt our loved ones.

These first five techniques will be that starting place.

1. Time out; This is a plan for removing yourself from a situation as soon as the first sign of anger or other strong emotions take place. You take this break and use it to practice the next four techniques so that you can come back and address the problem more constructively. To address the problem, not the person. To address the problem, not just your emotional response.
2. Rational thinking; This is a time-honored method to look at our thinking and learn how to think more rationally in order to calm ourselves down and address issues more clearly. We should all practice this every day. It should be a life style. But it is especially important to practice when we are taking a time out and need to think rationally and calmly. When we learn how to think rationally we have control over our lives. When

we have control over our lives, we have no need to control others. Anger, control, abuse and violence are, at their root, irrational behaviors, and a sign of thinking and/or living irrationally.

3. <u>Relaxation;</u> Our bodies play a big role in our reactions to events and learning how to calm our bodies down will help calm our brains down and help us think more clearly. We should make this part of our daily routine and especially when we are facing tension or a potentially explosive situation.

4. <u>Conflict management</u>; Now that you are thinking calmer and feeling calmer you can use conflict management techniques to plan a more constructive way to address the problem at the end of the time out. So that you can address the problem, and not the person. This is an especially good part of our daily routines to manage conflicts before they become big and potentially explosive.

5. <u>Relapse prevention</u>; In order to be able to stop problems before they get out of hand we need a plan. A plan for detecting well in advance situations in which the potential for anger or violence could occur, and addressing the problems before they arise. This can be a part, not only of your personal relapse plan, but something that you and your partner or future partners could use to find our when you are starting to slip, and not just wait until the conflict erupts.

LESSON ONE:

THE TIME OUT PLAN

WAC 388-60-0245 (8)

You can't have an argument if you aren't there. Arguments don't cause violence, abuse, or control. Arguments are about winning, winning by making the other person lose, by disempowering the other person, and winning is about control. So *wanting* to win, *wanting* to make the other person lose, *wanting* to control is what causes arguments and ultimately violence. However, arguments can be a ripe situation for things to escalate into violence, abuse or control. Consequently the first step has to be a plan to contain arguments so that they don't escalate into violence, abuse or control.

This is called a TIME OUT PLAN. It is a commitment you make to yourself, and with the knowledge of those around you, that, if you find yourself thinking, feeling, or acting in a way that might signal you are starting to get angry or escalate, you will say "Time Out" and take a specific kind of break. And, even more important, it is a commitment that if *they* feel you might be getting into that space, they can ask you to take a time out, that you will, and you will come back later and let them finish the discussion safely.

It is only when your loved ones feel empowered to set reasonable limits on your anger that they can feel safe enough to be with you. If they can't time you out, then you are not safe to be with them. If you question their right to time you out, you aren't a safe person to be with. It really is that simple; if you don't give your loved ones the right to set reasonable limits on your anger, in the form of a time-out, you are making the decision to be an unsafe person for them to be with. And, if it isn't safe for them to be with you, they will eventually want to not be with you. It's your choice.

This is not the same thing as *Copping Out* which is a way to avoid the issues, thoughts and feelings of the other person or *Walking Out* which is simply ending the discussion by leaving. It is a *Time Out*. This means that you agree that you are only going away far enough, and long enough, to calm down and then you will be back to finish the discussion calmly. The other person doesn't have to be reluctant to let you go because they have your written guarantee you will come back and let them finish if they want to. If you don't come back and finish the discussion they have no reason to trust that you'll come back so they'll be reluctant to let you take a time out. You won't have earned their trust yet.

There are several rules necessary for making it an effective, empowering time out.

1. <u>Always use precisely the same word for this event every single time</u>. It can be "I need a time out" or "I need one of those special breaks" or just making the "time out" sign from football or anything else you agree upon. By using the same word every time and not using that for anything else it reduces the chances of confusion. As long as you use exactly the same word every time.

2. <u>Never debate it</u>. If someone says "time out" to you, or its equivalent, take it. There will be plenty of time the rest of your life to discuss whether or not it was appropriate or not, and plenty of time to get the last word in later. But only one chance to prove you are trustworthy. If you deny the other person the right to ask for a time out, you have made yourself a person who isn't safe to be with. When you take this as an opportunity to demonstrate that you are a safe person to be with, you empower them, and you, to have a safe relationship that can last a long time.

3. <u>Be gone just long</u> enough for the adrenaline to go down, not so long that it becomes a punishment for the other person, and not so short that you don't both have a chance to calm down. Probably not less than ten minutes and not more than an hour unless you both agree that it is necessary.

4. <u>Go far enough</u> away that you can't see or hear each other, and thus don't escalate, but not so far that the other person wonders what you could be doing. A good rule is to leave the room you are in, but not the location. For example, let the other person stay in the room they are in and you go to another room, but don't leave home. Or, if you feel strongly about leaving the residence, be specific where you are going and where you won't go. For example don't go to a bar or a movie. Just go away long enough and far enough to calm down and then resume the discussion.

5. <u>Don't do anything other than calm down while you are gone.</u> Don't read a book or watch TV or anything else. Just sit and calm down. Most certainly don't obsess about how to get even.

6. <u>Always, *always*, **always** come back and give them the opportunity to finish the discussion</u>, no matter how many times you have to take a time out, unless the other person freely decides they don't want to finish it. Otherwise it is only a way to manipulate your way out of the discussion you're afraid you can't win. Remember, this is about empowering the other person, not about winning.

There is a TIME OUT PLAN following this lesson. Take it out, fill it out and, if you are still with a loved one, share it with them. If not, make it out *as if* you were still in a relationship. Ultimately you will need to have one with whomever you end up with.

You will notice a few things about it.

1. You can time yourself out,
2. They can time you out and
3. They can time themselves out.
4. You can't time them out. That would be controlling. A time out is supposed to be a better way of controlling yourself and empowering the other person, not a better or sneakier way to control the other person.

The first step in not being a controlling person is to control yourself, not other people. This is about controlling yourself, not about controlling them.

The second thing is that they are only signing that they have been informed, not that they are agreeing to anything. For the same reasons noted above, it is important that this be about self control, not about controlling others.

ASSIGNMENT ONE is to complete the Time-Out Plan for yourself and the person you are with. If you are alone, fill it out as if you were with someone. Bring the plan to group for feedback from the other members. Bring a copy for your chart, and keep one for your record toward the final inventory. If the other person doesn't wan to read it or sign it, that's okay. Let it go.

ASSIGNMENT ONE
TIME OUT PLAN

I have a problem with anger. I am trying to change that. I am showing you this plan to let you know what I will be doing to control that anger. This plan is a commitment I am making to you. You are not required to commit to anything.

I will be taking a time out when I feel I am angry or might become angry. Some of the signs, which tell me I might be getting angry, are _____

I will let you know that I am taking a time out by saying _____

When I take a time out I will be gone not less than _____ minutes and no longer than _____ minutes.

Places I go to time out will be _____

I promise that I won't go _____

I will use the time out only to calm myself down and become more rational. I won't engage in other activities. I won't avoid the problem or issue or topic.

I promise that after a time out I will come back and finish the discussion calmly, if you would like to finish the discussion. I won't use it to cut off or avoid a discussion.

You are also free to time me out if you feel I am becoming angry, violent, or controlling or if, for any other reason, you feel I need one. If you want me to take a time out you can say
_____

And I promise to follow the same steps I mentioned above.

If, for any reason, you want to take a time out yourself, all you have to do is to say
_____

I will not interfere with you taking a time out and I will respect your space and your feelings.

Name_____ Submitted ___/___/___

I acknowledge you shared this plan with me _____/___/___

LESSON TWO:

RATIONAL THINKING

WAC 388-60-0245 (!), (2)

<u>Our thoughts create our world.</u>

We begin the process of anger by *Thinking Angry*.

We live in a pretty neutral world. There really isn't much difference between bad milk and good yogurt except the name we put on it. Whether the Yankees winning the World Series is good or bad depends on which side you bet on. A pretty woman in the jungles of South America would meet a different standard than a pretty woman in Beverley Hills, and vice versa. Some people see a taco shell with an image of the Virgin Mary on it, and some people see a taco shell.

In fact, what science–and our own every day experience–has shown us repeatedly is that our brains don't know the difference between what we think and what is really happening. I can talk about delicious food until you start to salivate and get hungry, even though no food is actually present. I can watch a scary movie until I am scared out of my wits, my heart is racing and I am sweating, even though, in fact, there is no monster there.

I am reacting to what I think, more than to what is actually happening.

> A man, traveling in a rented car, has a flat tire far out in the country. He stops and opens the trunk, only to discover that there is a spare tire, but no jack.
>
> "This is terrible," he thinks. "Here I am stuck in the middle of nowhere with no jack! I'll be here forever!"
>
> Frustrated, he looks around and sees a farm house far away in the distance.
>
> "I can go there and borrow a jack from them," he tells himself, and feels better.
>
> He begins the long, hot walk, and begins to think again.
>
> "What if they don't have a jack?" he speculates. "What will I do then?" He began to worry again.
>
> "Worse, what if they have a jack and they won't loan it to me?" he thinks, and becomes angry. "I'd just have to tell them where to go, that's what I'd do! But then they'd get mad and they probably have a gun and they'd try to shoot me. Then I'd have to defend myself, and someone would probably get hurt. I'd get arrested and go to jail and my family would lose everything and I'd get gang raped on the cell block!"

He was so angry that, by the time he got to the farm house and the farmer opened the door, the salesman shouted "Keep your damn jack! You can just go to hell!"

This is an example of the way we react to what we think, not to what is actually there. This is a case of a person working himself into an anger outburst when, in fact, the only thing that happened was in his brain. This is called "self talk" and it means just what it says; the things we say when we talk to ourselves.

<u>Irrational self talk can keep us from being effective</u>

Most of our self-talk is accurate and useful;

- "It's time to go to work, if I get behind it will be hard to catch up."
- "I have to remember my wife's birthday. It's her 30th and that is special."
- "I don't understand why my son isn't getting better grades. I'll have to talk to him and find out."

These are reasonable, rational ways of thinking and lead us into constructive problem solving
But look what happens if we add a more extreme thought:

- "I have to go to work, even if I hate it. And I really hate it. It's awful that I have to go to work and I'll probably get in big trouble and be overwhelmed and never get caught up if I'm late."
- "Oh, God, not her birthday again; I always screw up and she doesn't like what I give her. This is such a hassle. Why aren't women easily pleased, like us guys are? And it's her 30th! If I don't do something special I'll never hear the end of it!"
- My son is a complete idiot! Why can't he get better grades? What the hell is wrong with him? I'm going to have a talk with him and make damn sure he understands the facts of life!"

What different reactions do you think these people would have with the two different ways of thinking about it? In the first case, they will be motivated to attack the problem. In the second case, they will probably react with anger and perhaps even inappropriate behavior because of their thinking;

1) Blameful thinking; "I hate it", "I hate work", "My son is a complete idiot", "What the hell is wrong with him?"
2) Awfulizing; "It's awful …", "This is such a hassle".
3) Future tripping and predicting negative outcomes; "I'll probably get in big trouble", "I'll be overwhelmed", "… never get caught up", "I'll never hear the end of it."
4) Speaking/thinking in extremes; "I always screw up", "… never hear the end of it …", "complete idiot",
5) Rehearsing conflicts that haven't happened yet; "If I don't do something special I'll never hear the end of it." "I'm going to have a talk with him and make damn sure he understands the fact of life."
6) Judgmental thinking: "My son is a complete idiot", "why aren't women easily pleased, like men are?"

Because of the disastrous quality of the thinking of the person in the second case, they will probably respond "as if" the disasters they were telling themselves actually were occurring.

- Instead of just going to work, they would respond "as if" it was the most horrible thing they could imagine and could have found themselves irritable, unhappy, and hard to get along with all day.
- Instead of just planning a nice birthday party, they would have responded "as if" their wife's upcoming birthday was a looming disaster.
- Instead of helping their son with his homework they could easily have erupted into a nightmarish struggle and even verbal abuse–or worse.

These sorts of thoughts are referred to as "irrational" in that if you think about it, they don't actually make sense.

For example, it isn't true when you say "I can't stand it" when, in fact, you have "stood it" without dying. The truth is that you really, really don't like it. But you can stand it. You are standing it.

Then there are the extreme words; "always", and "never". If someone *never* was nice to me, that would be pretty bad. If they were nice to me some of the time, and not nice a lot of the time, that's a whole different thing. If you *always* lied to me, literally never telling me the truth, that would be a real deal breaker. There would be no reason to be in a relationship. But, if the truth was that you periodically lied, even about many things, that's a different situation.

Again, it's not so much that the words we think and say to ourselves are *wrong*, but they are too much, too extreme, too disastrous, to be workable.

Beliefs

Another category of thoughts and self talk which can get us in trouble are our beliefs. We have to have beliefs, values, standards and ethics to guide us through the day. But we have to be open to reevaluating our beliefs and values as we mature and face new and different situations;

- We used to believe that Russians were our enemies, now they are our coworkers and allies.
- We used to have "careers" in which we would work for one company for our whole working lives and then retire from those companies; now we have many jobs, even many professions, over the course of our lifetimes, and companies come and go before we can retire.
- We used to believe that steak and potatoes were a healthy dinner. Now it's leafy greens and tofu.

There are a number of beliefs and groups of beliefs which often lead to family violence;

Beliefs about women;

- The role of a woman is different than the role of a man in a relationship
    - Women are weaker than men
    - Women should be subservient to men
    - Men should be the natural leaders
    - Women's jobs are less important than men's jobs
- Traits commonly associated with women are less desirable than traits commonly associated with being male;
    - Being nurturing and affectionate versus being tough and conditional
    - Being intuitive and emotional versus being logical
    - Trusting feelings at least as much as trusting thoughts
    - "Nesting"–shopping, decorating, making things pretty and nice–is less desirable than "hunting and gathering"–going out and making money and doing "guy things".
- The needs of women are frivolous and bothersome
    - The need for reassurance
    - The need to talk
    - The need to cuddle, be affectionate
    - The need to be close

Beliefs about relationships

- Once I am in a relationship it should stay the same forever and not require work
- Once I'm in a relationship I can do things I couldn't do with someone I wasn't in a relationship with, and I can get away with things I wouldn't get away with if I wasn't in a relationship.

- Once I'm in a relationship the other person "owes me". That means that they don't have a right to end the relationship unless I think it's a good reason. They have to stay in the relationship and "work it out", no matter what. And if they try to leave because they want to, I have a right to stop them.

Beliefs about provocation

- I can do things in anger that I wouldn't be able to get away with if I did them calmly.
- If someone provokes me it justifies what I do in return.
- I get to pick what I feel is provocative or not, and, once I decide it was provocation, I can do whatever I want and blame it on the other person for provoking me.
- The other person is at fault if I feel provoked by them, and I can do whatever I want to them if I can justify feeling provoked.
- If another person has wronged me I have the right to punish them.
- I shouldn't be held responsible for things I do in anger. It's the other person's fault for making me angry.

Ideas about life

- Life should be fair
- Other people should agree with my perceptions and ideas
- I should be valued for who I am, not what I do, and it's unbearable that I have to earn respect or change my behavior to be trusted.

The list is relatively endless. However the rule is still the same; if we do something that isn't successful or doesn't make sense or doesn't make things better, it is because we are not thinking correctly. The cure is not to make other people or circumstances change to meet our thoughts and expectations. The cure is to learn to correct our thinking.

Talking ourselves into being angry

Typically the steps we go through to use irrational thoughts and beliefs to make ourselves angry are;

1. I must get my way, no matter what.
2. I didn't get my way, and that's awful, I can't stand it.
3. It's your fault I didn't get my way.
4. That makes you the "bad guy". And, if you are the bad guy, that makes me the good guy, the victim.
5. You should be punished for being the bad guy and not letting me get my way.
6. That justifies me punishing you.

Learning how to correct our thinking.

Thinking is a skill and, like any other skill, we can learn to do it better and better over time, if we practice. If not, bad habits tend to get worse and we can get pretty sloppy.

We get what we get because we do what we do. We do what we do because we think what we think. If we want to get different, better results out of life, we have to look first at our thinking.

Evaluating our thinking

If we want to get better at thinking, so that we get better results in life, we have to first learn to evaluate our thinking.

What is the first step in evaluating anything we do? We ask, "AM I GETTING THE RESULTS I WANT OUT OF MYSELF?"

If you are getting the results you want out of yourself, out of your life, your relationships, your feelings and your behavior, great! But you probably wouldn't be reading this book, if that was the case.

If you aren't getting the results you want out of yourself, out of your life, then, instead of looking at the world and saying "what the heck is wrong with the world?" you need to look at yourself and ask "what is wrong with my thinking and problems solving? How am I out of synch with the way things work?"

In this world, what we think determines what we do, and what we do determines what we get. If we want to get something different, we have to do something differently. But we do what we do because we think what we think. If we want to get something different by doing something differently, we have to think differently.

What were you thinking when you did what you did which got you here? What were your errors of thinking?

It really is that simple. It just takes a lifetime to get it just right.

The only information anyone has with which to form an opinion of us is, is what we do. Whether they have known us our whole lives or have just met us. All they have to go on is what we do. If I want you to trust me and you don't, I can't blame you. That would be like a marksman blaming the target. I have failed to be trustworthy in your eyes. I can choose to leave or I can choose to learn from my mistakes and stay. Either way, it's my choice. It's not about you. It's about me. About my skill and/or my decision to stay.

So, if you are happy with your life in general, but you don't like the opinions or reactions of some of your loved ones, then that is the surest sign that you need to evaluate what you are doing that gets that reaction, and what are the thoughts which lead to the behavior which leads to the reaction.

<u>Thinking differently: Rational Counters</u>

A Rational Counter is the more realistic version of what we are telling ourselves.

For example, if I got angry at my wife for mentioning that we didn't have enough money, and my irrational thought was "damn it, she has no right to complain, I'm working as hard as I can", then what would be the logical counter?

First of all, she might not be complaining. She could easily just be telling the truth; it's hard to make ends meet these days. Is it true? Are you having trouble making ends meet the way she would like to have things work out? It's probably true.

Secondly, if she is telling the truth, as she knows it, do you have to take it personally? Do you have to take it as a personal attack? No, you don't have to take it personally. In that case the logical counter would be "it isn't personal, that's just the way it is. I'm working as hard as I can and we still need more money."

If so, then the rational counter would be "she's telling the truth, it *is* hard."

A rational counter doesn't have to be happy. Just rational. You probably won't be able to convince yourself to be happy that your wife is upset over the money. But you can handle it rationally. In fact, if you think about it rationally enough, you might just come up with a solution!

For the next assignment, go down the first column and list the things you did, the specific behaviors you did which were angry, controlling, abusive or violent and/or which got you here. For example; "I yelled at my wife and told her to go to hell if she didn't think I was doing a good enough job."

Then, in the next column, list the irrational thoughts you had, or the irrational self talk, which led to the behavior. For example; "I just can't stand it when she criticizes me; I can't stand it; I can't work any harder."

In the third column write down the rational counter which would led to more appropriate behavior. For example; "I agree with her, we don't have enough money and it sucks; but it's not personal; it's just dollars and cents."

ASSIGNMENT TWO
RATIONAL THINKING

WAC 388-60-0245 (1), (2)

What are the things I did which ultimately resulted in me needing to be in the program?	What are the irrational thoughts I used to talk myself into being angry or into doing something that hurt the other person?	These are the rational counters I could have used to talk myself down and will use in the future to talk myself down.

Name _____ Date completed___/___/___

LESSON THREE:

RELAXATION

In addition to anger being part of our thinking, anger is also a physical event. Feeling angry means many physical changes in our bodies and brains to prepare us to meet a physical attack. We use RELAXATION so that we don't *feel* angry, and then not *act* angry.

Our bodies affect what we are thinking and feeling, and our minds reflect what is happening in our bodies. It's a feedback loop. We use positive self talk to stop the cycle of anger in our minds, and we use relaxation to stop the part of the cycle which is happening in our bodies.

Physical tension is one of the ways our bodies prepare to attack an enemy or defend ourselves from an attack. Unfortunately, this system in our bodies evolved at a time when all of our threats and stresses were physical. This is unfortunate, because the vast majority of the stresses and threats we experience in modern life are not physical attacks. Mostly, they are emotional attacks, financial attacks, and interpersonal stresses. Those sorts of stresses and demands don't respond well to us defending ourselves physically.

Obviously, if you are attacked physically, a physical defense, such as freezing, fleeing, or fighting back, might be an expedient response. But that is rarely the case. If, however, the threat is that your boss is doing your annual evaluation, it would not be appropriate to attack him or her physically. If the stress is that your mother-in-law thinks you are a poor husband for her daughter, chasing her off with a stick isn't going to help your case.

We have to control our body's desire to respond physically to threats which aren't actually physically life threatening, or we'll end up with more problems. For example, being in this program.

This response of our body to a perceived threat consists of three parts.

First, when we perceive a threat, our brains tell our bodies that this is a dangerous situation and that we should increase our adrenalin level so that we are stronger, faster, and more aggressive in fighting off this threat.

This creates what is known as the ***Freeze-Fight-Flight Syndrome.***

> *Freeze* When we are faced with physical danger our first response is to do nothing; to freeze, or "play possum" to draw as little attention to ourselves as possible, to avoid getting hurt. Sometimes this appears as giving in or being obedient to the threat in order to minimize damage to ourselves.
>
> *Fight.* If we can destroy the thing we feel is threatening us, we do.
>
> *Flight* If we can't destroy the threat, we escape it by running away.

All three of these states create adrenalin, cortisone, and other hormones and substances which create physical preparedness, physical strength, and physical tension. Unfortunately, as we become more physically tense, our brains interpret this physical tension as indicating there is more risk. Our brains become more vigilant and look harder for the danger. And, the harder we look, the more we find. Consequently, the more we become tense, the more angry and defensive we become, and thus we become more tense. It becomes a vicious cycle.

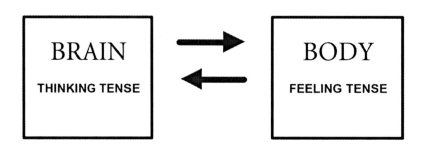

This tension consists of

- Tightened muscles
- Fast, abrupt, shallow breathing
- Increased blood pressure, increased heart rate
- Tightened capillaries

To break this cycle so that we don't **Feel Angry** we need to practice RELAXATION.

- Practice this at least once per day, at least ten or fifteen minutes at a time. You should do this so that you become skilled at relaxing, so that in times of tension you can do it effectively.
- You should also take a few moments to relax prior to stressful events, such as facing your boss, paying the bills, or discussing difficult issues.
- Definitely you need to do it whenever you are taking a TIME OUT and before and after each time you use CONFLICT MANAGEMENT.

RELAXATION

Do this at least once per day, at least ten or fifteen minutes per occasion, so that you become skilled at doing it. The purpose is to stop the *Feeling Angry* part of the cycle of *Feeling Angry-Thinking Angry–Acting Angry.*

1. Pick the right time and place.
    a. It should be a place where you can sit or lie quietly without distractions or interruptions.
    b. It should be a time when you aren't so tired that you are at risk of falling asleep. That's not a bad side effect, but you should be awake for the practice part of it.
2. Sit or lie comfortably.
    a. You should sit or lie in a place where you can completely relax without falling over.
    b. Relax any unneeded muscles. Untighten your fists, relax your shoulders and face.
    c. Don't fold your arms or legs or cross your feet; this could cut off your circulation.
3. Breathing.
    a. This always begins and ends with breathing. This is the quickest, easiest way to stop the cycle of tension and anger, once you master it, and it really isn't hard to master.
    b. Breathe in with your nose and out with your mouth.
    c. Breathe with your stomach, not with your chest.
    d. Breathe deeply and rhythmically. This called "square breathing".
        i. Breathe in to a count of five
        ii. Hold it for a count of five
        iii. Let it out for a count of five
        iv. Leave it out for a count of five
        v. Repeat
    e. Concentrate on feeling the whole course of your breathing as it goes in your nose, through your nose, down your windpipe, all the way through your lungs, back out your windpipe, and out your mouth. Try to learn as much as possible about your breathing. Concentrate on just that one thing.
4. Thinking.
    a. Don't think in words. Our brains are imprisoned by an army of poorly trained word monsters! Try to stop listening to them. Try to just let them become background noise. Don't pay attention to those word thoughts. Don't judge them; just don't pay attention.
        i. If you find yourself thinking in words, don't make a big deal out of it, because if you do, you'll just think in more words. For example, "Darn, there I am thinking in words again!"
        ii. Instead of fighting your words, just let them go and replace them with thinking about your breathing.
        iii. Don't be hard on yourself, this is about relaxing. Even people skilled at relaxation can seldom go more than a few seconds without thinking in words, and then letting them go and going back to thinking about their breathing.
5. Your muscles.
    a. Your muscles are the container of your tension. When you tighten your muscles your muscle cells burn sugar to get the energy to tighten up. That creates waste material which is toxic. That's why your muscles hurt after hard exercise. Under normal circumstances, after we work our muscles, we relax them and our blood streams carry away the toxins. When we are tense and don't relax, the blood doesn't get through as well, and the toxins stay there and hurt, which makes us tighten our muscles more.
    b. We have to
        i. Relax our muscles
        ii. Relax the capillaries which carry the blood
        iii. Stay relaxed.

    c. We do this by systematically tightening and then suddenly relaxing each muscle group in turn two or three times to relax the muscles, dilate the capillaries, and let the blood bring in oxygen and take out toxins. This feels good.
    d. Tighten and relax each of these muscle groups in turn, while continuing to square breathe and think about your breathing.
        i. Your toes
        ii. Your feet
        iii. Your legs
        iv. Your stomach
        v. Your chest
        vi. Your biceps and triceps
        vii. Your forearms and fists
        viii. Your shoulders
        ix. Your neck
        x. Your forehead
        xi. Your eyes
        xii. Your lips and cheeks
        xiii. Your tongue.
6. Once you have relaxed your body, and you are square breathing regularly, just enjoy the feeling of relaxation. Learn as much as possible about how it feels. Your body very likely will feel warmer and heavier. Bask in this feeling for ten minutes or so. Continue to catch yourself thinking in words and just gracefully letting them go without making a big deal out of it. Just let the words become background noise.
7. When you are ready to rejoin the world, do it very slowly and gradually, and try to take some of the relaxation with you for the rest of the day.

ASSIGNMENT THREE
USING RELAXATION

When were the times, in the past week, that I practiced relaxation when it wasn't a part of a time out or conflict?

How well did I manage to relax? _____
_____

What could I do better or differently next time? _____
_____

When were the times I relaxed, in the last week, in order to prevent getting angry or upset? _____
_____

How well did it work? _____
_____

What could I do better next time? _____
_____

When were the times I used relaxation, in the last week, during a time out or during a conflict? _____
_____

How well did it work? _____
_____

What could I do better next time? _____
_____

Name _____ Date completed ___/___/___

LESSON FOUR:

CONFLICT MANAGEMENT

So far, we have learned how to take Time-Outs when we are becoming angry, then how to talk ourselves down with rational thinking and self talk, and then how to physically calm ourselves down with relaxation. Now we are ready to address the conflict.

Conflict is a simple reality of life. You want to go to Albertson's because they have a better price on milk, I want to go to Safeway because it's closer and we can save gas. Life is full of little conflicts; conflicts are just a part of life.

We live in a world where there is a limited amount of time and space, and sometimes we just can't do two opposite things. We can't spend the time and money to go on a vacation if we spend the time and money working on the house. You want to share your feelings, and I don't want to feel blamed.

We can't avoid conflict, but we can manage it so that it doesn't become a heated conflict where anger or violence could occur. This is no different than learning how to use a toilet or balance a check book. It's just a part of growing up. When we manage something well, it doesn't become an emergency.

Also, we need to learn how to manage our conflicts in ways which are fair, and not abusive or controlling. Ways which can actually bring us closer to the other person and improve the quality of our lives. Each conflict is an opportunity to create a stronger, safer, better relationship.

You should use CONFLICT MANAGEMENT as soon as you realize that a conflict might happen or might be happening, or after taking a TIME OUT. The goal of CONFLICT MANAGEMENT is

    1) To take control of the conflict before it controls you.

    2) To keep the conflict within certain non-violent limits and address the *problem* rather than attack *each other*.

    3) To end it as quickly as possible, without abuse, control, or violence.

CONFLICT MANAGEMENT consists of the following six steps;

1) **_Identify_** that this is a conflict, and not just an ordinary discussion, by identifying the cues, such as raised voices, negative emotions, etc.
2) Make five key **_decisions_**;
    a. <u>Do I want to be here?</u> Do I want to be here *now?*—if not, you can *time out, reschedule,* or *disengage and leave.* You don't have to stick around for every conflict. In some cases, it's wiser to let it pass.

b. If you do decide to continue in the conflict, decide <u>what is this conflict really about</u>? Most of the time, conflicts, once you think about it, really aren't about anything more than just being frustrated and angry. Sometimes the two people in the conflict are actually arguing about slightly different things, and really aren't disagreeing at all;
   i. <u>What do they want</u>? By that, I don't mean what is the *most* that they want. I'm asking what is the bare minimum which will satisfy them enough to end the conflict.
   ii. <u>What do I want</u>? What is the *minimum* I will settle for to leave this conflict.
   iii. <u>How far am I willing to go</u> to get it?—establish the price you are willing to pay for what you want. Sometimes what you are willing to do to "win" a conflict is a lot less than you end up paying. Is this conflict really worth it? How far are you willing to go to make a point? Are you willing to risk losing a relationship on this subject? Are you willing to risk going to jail? Losing a job? A friend?

3) <u>**Prepare**</u> yourself mentally, physically and logistically.
   a. **Mentally** use positive self-talk. Find a way to calm yourself and get focused on the problem, not the person. Make a plan about what you want and how you will say it.
   b. **Physically** relax, make sure you aren't making things worse by being tense or threatening.
   c. **Logistically;** Is this the right time and place for this conflict? Make sure that there are no distractions, preferably no audience, and both parties are in the right condition to have this discussion.

4) <u>**Execute**</u> your plan.
   a. **Acknowledge** the legitimacy of the other person's position. **Validate** their feelings and personal experience. This isn't the same thing as agreeing, only letting them know that they have been heard in a polite way. Use active listening and paraphrasing until they understand that you really have heard them. Don't just say "I understand". Actually state what you think their position is. For example "I understand that you feel disrespected and ignored when I make decisions without involving you, and I agree that it was a rude thing for me to do".
   b. **State** your position in the shortest, simplest manner;
      i. "<u>When … happens.…</u>" What is it that you are reacting to? Be specific. Be sure you are talking about the problem, not the person. For example; "I'm not objecting to you being angry; I'm just talking about having less than a minute to keep the mortgage check from bouncing."
      ii. "<u>I think.…</u>" What are the things you are thinking, what is your self talk which leads to your feelings? Remember, it isn't *what happens* that causes our feelings, it's *what we tell ourselves* that causes the emotional reaction. For example " When that happens I think we are handling our finances too chaotically, we're playing everything too close to the line."
      iii. "<u>I feel.…</u>" what are the emotions you are having? "I feel really confused and frustrated and frightened about our futures."
      iv. "<u>I would like to.…</u>" Be behavioral, simple, and specific. State what the outcome is that you want in a polite, non-threatening manner. "For example; "I'd like us to sit down with the budget and come up with a system for keeping track of our finances and paying our bills."
         1. Make sure that it is;
            a. non-blaming
            b. non-threatening
            c. negotiable, do-able, and practical
            d. non-provocative
            e. attacks the **problem,** not the **person**
      v. "<u>And in return I would like to offer</u> …" It's not polite to ask for something and not offer anything in return. Give something back. For example; "And in return I'll promise to never make a decision again without asking your or consulting our plan first."
   c. Having said your piece ***let them respond*** and use active listening, rephrasing, and any other means you have to ***help them feel heard! Validate them!***

5) <u>**Start over**</u> and continue the process until either

a. you have met your goal or
b. you have met the price you set in step two; don't go further than you intended to go
6) **_Take a break_** to reflect on what you did well and reward yourself and the other person for a job well done. Do something nice.

EXAMPLES

Example #1. John comes home and finds his wife distraught because, on the way home from work, her car ate the head gasket, and it would cost more to fix the car than it would be worth after the repair. She is weeping and screaming that it is all his fault, because they don't have enough money to buy her a decent car. She is demanding that they get a new car right away, because she can't get to work without a car. John is on the verge of telling her that it's all her fault and she has no right to be angry.

WRONG WAY

John tells her it isn't his fault, and demands that she stop yelling at him, that it isn't his fault that they don't have enough money to replace her car, it's her fault because she doesn't make enough at her job. They yell back and forth until he grabs her, shakes her, and tells her to shut up.

RIGHT WAY

John realizes that she is upset. He also realizes that he, too, is upset. He waits until she gets it off her chest, then holds her and comforts her. He realizes that her upset is just as real as his own frustration and disappointment, and realizes that she needs to hear that there is some hope, that there is a plan. Both of them want the same thing; a plan.

He sits down, facing her, and says;

1. Acknowledge the legitimacy of her position; "Honey, I understand what you are saying. You are right, you can't get to work without a car and that is completely true. You have a right to feel upset."
2. State what you are reacting to; "We are between a rock and a hard spot; you genuinely need a car and we genuinely don't have the money. It sounds like, when that happens, you feel like I'm the bad guy."
3. State what your self talk is, what your thoughts are; "When we are in a jam like this, I think that this is the sort of thing that can break up our marriage, if we end up on opposite sides on this problem.
4. State what you are feeling; "I feel really sad and far away from you, and I want to be closer to you, and frustrated with our situation. I want us to work out solutions together."
5. State what you want: "I would like us to work together to make a plan. At the very least, you drop me off at work tomorrow and you can use the car, and we can do it that way, alternating who gets the car and who uses the bus, until we can find an affordable used car someplace."
6. State what you are offering in return: "In return I will work as hard as possible with you to get you into a car as soon as possible. And, after that, get our finances under control."

Example #2. Henry reads the call log from the cell phone bill, and discovers that his wife has been calling her sister, whom Henry feels is a "bad influence" on her, several times a day. In the past she has accused Henry of being too controlling, and he wants his wife to stop talking to her sister. He confronts her with what he has discovered. She is also angry with him for checking up on her, and demands that he let her talk to whoever she wants to talk to.

WRONG WAY. Yell at her and tell her to shut up and stop talking to her damn sister.

RIGHT WAY.

1. Acknowledge the legitimacy of her position; "You have a right to be angry at me for checking up on you. I have no right to do that."
2. State what you are reacting to: "When I see you talking to your sister that much …"

3. <u>State what you are thinking</u>: "I think that you are talking to her about me and that there is something going on that I don't know about …"
4. <u>State what you are feeling</u>: "And I feel really scared and threatened. I don't want to lose you, and I feel sometimes like I'd do almost anything to keep you from leaving me."
5. <u>State what you want</u>: "I'd like you to feel safe sharing your feelings with me about what you feel about me. I'd like you to feel safe telling me what you think I should hear, or what if is that I'm not understanding."
6. <u>State what you offer in return</u>: "If you do that, I'll promise to not yell or judge or get upset about it, and if I start to get upset I promise to take a time out. Most of all, I won't try to control who you talk to, and I'll never check the phone logs or check up on you in any way again."

Use this format each time you detect a conflict. Below is a form called a CONFLICT MANAGEMENT LOG. Make a lot of copies for your use at home. You use this each time there is a potential conflict and you use CONFLICT MANAGEMENT to prevent it from getting out of hand. Use this even on small conflicts; conflicts your partner might not even think are conflicts. This is an ongoing practice and it's separate from the homework assignment, below. If you do it long enough, it can even become automatic.

Each week, when you check in at group, one of the questions is whether or not you used conflict management that week and, if so, how well you used it. This is what that refers to.

Assignment Four, Conflict Management, uses a Conflict Management Log to evaluate what you did ***in the event or events which brought you here***, and what you should have or could have done better.

CONFLICT MANAGEMENT LOG FOR USE AT HOME

HOW WELL DID I READ THE SIGNS THAT THIS WAS A CONFLICT? _____

_____

HOW WELL DID I UNDERSTAND WHAT IT WAS ABOUT? _____

_____

HOW WELL DID I EVALUATE MY GOAL OR WHAT I WANTED TO GET OUT OF THE CONFLICT? _____

_____

HOW WELL DID I DO AT EVALUATING WHAT THE OTHER PERSON WANTED?

_____

HOW WELL DID I **PREPARE MYSELF MENTALLY**? _____

HOW WELL DID I **PREPARE MYSELF PHYSICALLY**? _____

1. WHAT WORDS DID I USE TO ACKNOWLEDGE THEIR POSITION AND HOW WELL DID I DO?

"_____"

HOW DID I STATE MY POSITION, AND HOW WELL DID IT WORK?

2. "WHEN _____"

3. "I THINK _____"

4. "I FEEL _____"

5. "I WOULD LIKE _____"

6. "AND I OFFER _____"

OVERALL, HOW WELL DID IT WORK, AND WHAT COULD I IMPROVE ON?

_____

LESSON FOUR
CONFLICT MANAGEMENT IN THE EVENT WHICH LED TO ME BEING HERE

HOW SHOULD I HAVE READ THE SIGNS THAT THIS WAS A CONFLICT? _____
_____

WHAT WAS IT REALLY ALL ABOUT? _____
_____
_____

WHAT SHOULD MY GOAL HAVE BEEN FOR RESOLVING THE THE CONFLICT? _____
_____
_____

WHAT DID THE OTHER PERSON WANT? _____

HOW SHOULD I HAVE PREPARED MYSELF MENTALLY? _____

HOW SHOULD I HAVE PREPARED MYSELF PHYSICALLY? _____

WHAT WORDS SHOULD I HAVE USED TO ACKNOWLEDGED THEIR POSITION?
_____ "

HOW SHOULD I HAVE STATED MY POSITION?

2. "WHEN _____ "

3. "I THINK _____ "

4. "I FEEL _____ "

5. "I WOULD LIKE _____ "

6. "AND I OFFER _____ "

Name _____ Date Submitted ___/___/___

LESSON FIVE:

RELAPSE PREVENTION PLAN

WAC 388-60-0245 (11)

Anger, control, abuse, and violence don't just fall out of the sky and land on our heads. There is a series of events leading up to any act of anger, control, abuse or violence. A series of thoughts, feelings, circumstances, actions and conditions. It is easier to *prevent* anger, control, abuse and violence than it is to *stop* them. The earlier in the process we catch the progression into a relapse, the easier it is to prevent it.

- <u>Have you ever had a bad day?</u> A day when nothing seemed to work out right? When everything hurt and it took a lot of energy to not say or do something inappropriate, even something abusive? When you felt like you were about to explode? When everything looked threatening, bad or just plain irritating?

- <u>Have you ever had a good day?</u> A day when nothing went all that wrong, a day when you felt able to deal with life on life's terms? A day when, no matter what the stressor was that came your way, you were up to it, you could handle it?

- <u>Have you ever had a good day *after* a bad day?</u> And then looked back on the things that set you off on the bad day, and wondered what the big deal was?

The *things*, the events and circumstance that happened to you, didn't change from the bad day to the good day and back again. The *things* stayed the same. What made the difference are our attitudes. The things we tell ourselves. The things that set us off aren't what set us off. The difference is in our heads. The things we are thinking, feeling, and dealing with.

That is an example of the importance of the events, actions, thoughts and circumstances leading up to our acts of anger, control, abuse and violence. In the right frame of mind, we are sane, and realize that there is nothing worth getting upset about. In the wrong frame of mind, we can justify, rationalize, or excuse being angry, controlling, abusive or violent.

That's where a RELAPSE PREVENTION PLAN comes in. In it, we take the time to itemize everything that happened, everything that went through our minds, which led up to the anger, control, violence or abuse which landed us here, so that we detect it–and prevent it–before it's too late.

To begin making a RELAPSE PREVENTION PLAN we need to look at the patterns, thoughts and circumstances which have led up to relapses in the past, so that we can know how to prevent them in the future.

It is important that I emphasize as much as possible that we are talking about *any* kind of relapse. Not just a "hitting" type of relapse. Any act of anger, control, abuse or violence is a relapse. So whether we relapse by hitting someone, or by looking like we are going to hit them, we are still sending them the message that they are at risk. We are still controlling them through fear. A "big" relapse, or a "little" relapse, shows that we still have the thoughts, beliefs and responses which can lead to anger, control, abuse or violence. Any relapse sends the message that we haven't changed yet.

So let's look at *all* of your past relapses, so that we can, hopefully, prevent *all* of your future relapses. And look as far as possible *before* the relapse when collecting ideas about your relapses. Remember, the earlier in the process you catch yourself, the more easily you can prevent a relapse.

We are going to look at the following categories of things that might lead to a relapse. But each person is unique. There could be many others that are important in your situation, in your life. So feel free to add any categories you feel are relevant.

Situations

We are creatures of habits. When we are faced with a situation we have experienced before, we tend to respond the same way we did before. Most people report that many of their relapses happen in situations that are similar. This includes situations which are only symbolically like the other ones. For example, family dinners. There might be many different dinners at many different houses with many different combinations of families. But they are all family dinners, and we may tend to respond to all of them the same way, or to some kinds of family dinners in similar ways.

Common examples include;

- Changes in your life, such as the birth of a child, a child growing up, the death of a loved one, the end of a job, moving, increases or decreases in income, ending a relationship, or starting a relationship.
- Certain times, like summer, Christmas vacation, Superbowl, or the anniversaries of significant events, such as the anniversary of the first offense, or tax time.
- Specific kinds of conflicts, such as paying the bills, paying taxes, deciding what to do about the kids, being reminded of past offenses, or having to set limits with your children.
- Specific circumstances, such as trying to repair your car, your partner having friends over who stay too late, or visitation exchanges.
- An external crisis, such as a flood, a fire, a car breaking down.
- Something of symbolic significance to past events.

Conditions

This includes conditions in yourself as well as in the people around you.

- You or the other person being hungry, angry, lonely or tired–the H.A.L.T. rule.
- You or the other person using drugs or alcohol.
- You or the other person being ill or in pain.
- Too much noise, too much going on, too much chaos, too many people in the house.
- Changes in your mood or the mood of the other person. For example, either of you
    o Becoming depressed or becoming more depressed.
    o Becoming more agitated or irritable.
    o Increases or decreases in sleep or appetite.

- o   Obvious signs of being unhappy, such as complaining more, frequent crying.
- Isolation, withdrawing from friends, family, or social supports.

Thoughts, Beliefs, Self Talk

Remember, external things don't control your feelings or actions. It's the way that you interpret those events that controls how you feel or what you do about it.

- Thinking judgmentally or mentally labeling or calling the other person or people names.
  - o   "That #$%^&*(!"
  - o   "What kind of idiot would…."
- Assuming motives for the other person or people.
  - o   "They must really think I'm stupid."
  - o   "They are out to get me."
- Entitlement or selfishness
  - o   "I deserve better."
  - o   "I don't deserve this crap."
  - o   "Screw them, I want what I want."
  - o   Not thinking about the needs and feelings of the other person or people involved.
- Resentment (this is a huge one!) or ruminating (dwelling on negative thoughts, past events, etc.)
- Rehearsing conflicts or future or potential fights or arguments in your head.

Things that you say

- Using an angry or threatening or condescending tone of voice with the other person or other people.
- Using judgmental words with the other person or other people.
  - o   "What a stupid thing to say …"
  - o   "Your problem is that you are lazy …"
  - o   "What a load of crap …"
  - o   "Obviously, this isn't important to you or you would have done XYZ …"
- Using "challenging" words with the other person or other people.
  - o   "Oh yea? You think so?"
  - o   "Prove it."
  - o   "I don't have to answer to you."
  - o   "You don't mean it …"
- Verbal/emotional abuse
  - o   "I never loved you anyhow."
  - o   "No wonder you don't have any friends."
  - o   "Up yours."
  - o   Swearing
  - o   Yelling.
- Threats
  - o   "Oh yea? See how you like it when you're living on the street."
  - o   "Any other man would just beat you up right now."
  - o   "If you don't _____ I will ____."
  - o   "If you _____ I will _____."
  - o   "That's it, I've had it!"
  - o   "What would your friends think if they knew ___ about you."
  - o   "You're an unfit parent and I'll get the kids."

Sexuality

Our sexuality is a very delicate part of our relationships, and can be a very good early warning sign that things are starting to go wrong.

- Changes in your sexuality, especially decreases in either your sexual desires or theirs.
- Dissatisfaction on the part of either of you about your sexuality.
- Sex becoming mechanical, not truly making love, not truly the connection between your souls and bodies.
- Either of you having an affair or thinking about it.
- Refusing sex.
- Forcing sex.
- Doing sexual things, such as using pornography, if the other person doesn't want us to do it, and we do it anyhow.
- Withdrawing sexually.
- Making negative sexual comments about the other person, for example, "Because you don't turn me on, because you're overweight …" or by your actions implying that you don't find the other person sexy or even that they disgust you, or that your sexual problems are because of them.
- Not being romantic.
- Arguing about sex, sexuality, or gender.

Actions, what you do

- Obviously any act of unwanted touching
    - Push, shove, shake, hold, grab, finger-to-the-chest, etc.
    - Throwing things at the other person or in their direction.
- Property damage
    - Hitting "things" such as punching walls or hitting tables
    - Throwing things near in the vicinity of the other person, but not at them.
    - Breaking things that are of significance to the other person, such as special pictures.
- Your actions
    - Waving your arms or acting agitated or threatening.
    - Pacing, gesturing, making angry faces.

What you don't do

- Not coming back from taking time outs.
    - Coming back, but not bothering to resolve anything.
- Withdrawing emotionally or physically from the other person or the family.
    - Physically staying away from the home.
    - If at home, spending more time in the den, garage, back room, etc. without the family.
    - Not being involved with the family discussions or activities.
    - Not being involved in the activities of the kids or taking care of the kids.
- "Forgetting" to do important thinks or things that you have promised to do.

Increases in compulsive or addictive behaviors or relapses in those areas.

There are many forms of compulsive or addictive behavior which are closely linked to anger, control, abuse and violence. Any relapses in those areas can signal getting ready to relapse. This includes

- Starting such a behavior
- Doing those behaviors in spite of the wishes or well being of your loved ones or dependents.
- Increasing doing any of them.
- Switching from one compulsive addictive behavior to another, such as switching from alcohol to food, from sex to religion, from gambling to the stock market.

The risk markers here can be changes in your use of these behaviors, or on the part of a loved one. The risk is still the same. The most common compulsive or addictive behaviors include but aren't limited to;

- Alcohol
- Drugs
- Compulsive or addictive sexual behavior, such as pornography, affairs, or prostitutes, when doing so is either against the wishes of your significant other, or without their knowledge.
- Gambling, which includes playing the stock market in ways your significant other either doesn't know or doesn't consent to.
- Food addictions or eating disorders.

Anything else

We are all unique. What are the signs and symptoms which you have noticed in your life which correlated with relapses? What haven't we thought of yet?

The RELAPSE PLAN itself is broken down into two levels.

1. Signs that I am about to have a relapse any moment now and I have to take a time out.
2. Long range signs that I am working my way back to the frame of mind or lifestyle which could eventually lead me to becoming angry, controlling, abusive or violent again, and I need to change what I am doing before I get there.

For each section you will need to record the signs and symptoms of the relapse and what you will plan to do about it.

Signs and symptoms of a pending relapse	What you are going to do to prevent or stop the relapse
Situations	
Conditions	
Thoughts, beliefs, or self talk.	
Things that I say	
Changes in our sexuality	
Actions–what I do or leave undone	
Other things that relate to my relapses	

If, for example, your relapses tend to come at times when you are especially depressed about your life or your job, a good relapse plan would be for you to tell your significant others that you are becoming more depressed and then start using resources, such as friends, counselors, career planners, etc. to start addressing those issues before you become more depressed and angry.

Another example is a relapse in compulsive addictive behavior. If you are a recovering alcoholic, drinking or relapsing into alcoholic thinking or alcoholic behavior would be a sure sign. The relapse plan would be to talk to your sponsor and go to more AA meetings. Perhaps even consider a brief inpatient treatment program.

One of the most important parts of a relapse plan, especially the long range relapse plan, is that you should set up and maintain a support system which supports non-violence. The friends, family and resources which can give you the feedback to know when you are slipping back and who can give you the emotional support to not get there. Friends, family, a minister, priest or rabbi, a church or temple you feel good about, an AA home group and sponsor you trust, a counselor you and your family feel good about, or a best friend you can rely upon. These should especially be people who support non-violence, non-sexism, people who practice in their own lives peaceful practices and have peaceful relationships themselves.

Be sure to include them in your relapse plan. Call on them if the signs and symptoms of a relapse, especially a long range relapse, begin to creep up. Talk to them, take their advice, as long as they don't justify abuse, control, or violence.

ASSIGNMENT FIVE
RELAPSE PREVENTION PLAN

WAC 388-60-0245 (11)

What are the immediate signs that I am currently relapsing and what is my relapse prevention plan for each of them?

Signs and symptoms that I am about to relapse or am currently relapsing	What I am going to do to stop the relapse in its tracks.
Situations	
Conditions	
Thoughts, beliefs, or self talk.	
Things that I say	
Changes in our sexuality	
Actions—what I do or leave undone	

LONG RANGE RELAPSE PREVENTION PLAN

Signs and symptoms that I am slipping back into the frame of mind or lifestyle which precedes my relapses	What I am going to do to prevent the relapse and get back on track
Situations	
Conditions	
Thoughts, beliefs, or self talk.	
Things that I say	
Changes in our sexuality	
Actions–what I do or leave undone	
Other things that relate to my relapses	

Who are the people and the resources to be my non-violence support group? _____

_____

Name _____ Date submitted ___/___/___

CHAPTER THREE

DOMESTIC VIOLENCE

ASSIGNMENT SIX: VIOLATION

The root word of violence is to *violate*. Before we can learn about violence, we have to understand what it is, how it works, how it feels.

Have you ever felt **violated**? Write down a few of the times you have felt **violated**. Write down what, specifically, happened which caused you to feel **violated**.

I felt violated when _____

_____

What do these things have in common? For most of us we feel violated when our rights, needs, and feelings have been imposed upon against our will. When we have been

- Robbed
- Cheated
- Lied to
- Disrespected
- Molested
- Discriminated against

We all like making love, but the difference between making love and being raped or molested is consent. We feel violated when we are forced to do something against our will or in way that violates our rights, needs, or feelings.

The difference between loaning someone some money and being robbed is the same thing: consent. If you ask me if you can borrow some money from me and I agree to it and loan it to you, then that is okay. But if you just take it from me, or take it from me under false pretenses, then it is stealing. I have been violated. For example if you tell me that you want to borrow the money to pay rent or buy medicine and I agree to it under those terms, then it is okay. But if, really, you are using the money to gamble or get high, then you have violated me.

When I was violated I felt _____

_____

When I was violated I did _____

_____

The following people have told me or shown me that they felt I had violated them; _____

_____

_____

The things I did which made them feel violated were_____

_____

The things which I did in the current situation which violated the other person were; _____
_____

If that had happened to me I would have felt _____
_____

When I did it to them it made them feel _____
_____

What should I have done which would have been more appropriate? What would have been the opposite of violating them? _____
_____

My inadequacies which motivated me to violate them was _____
_____

My plan for fixing those inadequacies is _____
_____
_____

The apology I owe them is _____
_____
_____

The amends I owe them are _____
_____

Name _____ Date submitted ___/___/___

LESSONS SEVEN THROUGH NINETEEN:

WHAT IS DOMESTIC VIOLENCE?

WAC 388-60-0245 (3)

This is the beginning of a rather long lesson, followed by several assignments. When you do the following assignments, you will be expected to identify each of the forms of control, abuse and violence which you have done, one category at a time. There may be other forms of control, abuse and violence, which you have done, which didn't specifically get mentioned in this lesson. However, be a good detective. Find out the forms of abuse which apply to what you did in your particular case.

Each assignment consists of

1. Taking inventory of the forms of abuse and/or control you have used in the category being discussed in that section.
2. The thoughts, beliefs and values which you used to rationalize that behavior.
3. The effect it had on the other person, and an explanation of the empathy you feel for them.
4. Your inadequacies which led to you using control, abuse or violence instead of dealing with those issues in a mature manner.
5. What you should have done differently.
6. The apology and amends you owe the other person for what you did.
7. The amends you have made that week, unless you are not allowed to have contact with that person or "when to do so would cause more harm".

The following sections will define control, abuse and violence and will explain each of the seven categories above.

1. WHAT ARE ABUSE, VIOLENCE, AND CONTROL?

Now, to begin the lesson plan about what violence is.

Violence is a large category of behaviors which
- Violate the rights, needs, feelings, or property of another person
    - Against their will, or
    - In a way they can't meaningfully resist
- Which controls them through
    - Fear of consequences
    - Fear of force
    - Misuse of power

The following table FORMS OF CONTROL, ABUSE, AND VIOLENCE illustrates the wide range of things that are violent according to this definition.

This table shows several things about violence
1. There are many forms of violence, not just physical. Anything that hurts another person or controls them against their will can be violent, abusive or controlling.
2. Violence can be PROGRESSIVE. That is, it can start at the INCONSIDERATION level of violence, such as ignoring the other person's needs, and then get worse over time, up to hitting them or hurting them, at the DESTRUCTION level.
3. There is always an ALTERNATIVE to the use of control, abuse, or violence.

FORMS OF CONTROL, ABUSE, AND VIOLENCE

Form of abuse, control, or violence	Inconsideration	Rejection	Destruction	Non-abusive Appropriate Alternatives
PHYSICAL ASSAULT	Allow harm to happen, accidents, brushing aside, unwanted touching	Push, shove, shake, reject reasonable requests and limits	Hit, kick, use of weapons, knocking down, causing injuries	Physical respect and comfort
SEXUAL ABUSE	Failure to respond to reasonable needs and limits, being inconsiderate or self serving	Refusal to respond to reasonable needs, rejecting limits, being forceful or humiliating	Forced sex, sexual humiliation to the point of interfering with their ability to function sexually or feel good about their sexuality	Sexual respect and intimacy, creating an atmosphere of comfort, dignity, and sexual fulfillment.
GENDER ABUSE	Indulging in personal, cultural, or religious stereotypes about gender and gender roles, taking advantage of gender differences	Requiring, or expecting, that the other person should fulfill your gender expectations or fulfill tasks that you decide are gender specific. Gender related jokes or cruelty	Forcing the other person into roles or activities based upon your gender definition, belittling their gender, discrimination based upon their gender, making them gender prisoners	Genuine equality of the sexes, respecting the rights, needs and feelings of all genders and gender orientations in an atmosphere of trust and safety.
EMOTION-AL ABUSE	Not taking the other person's feelings into account, being inconsiderate, ignoring them	Depreciating them as a person, belittling their contribution or value, making fun of them, not listening. Stalking, violating court orders, unwanted contact	Humiliation, degradation, causing embarrassment, depression, suicide, mental illness, poor self-esteem.	Praise, encouragement, emotional support, valuing them, acknowledging them.
VERBAL ABUSE	Bad language, name calling, labels	Ridicule, rudeness, and sarcasm. Yelling	Screaming, assaulting their value as a person to the point of causing emotional or psychological damage	Using words to calm and sooth, creating an atmosphere of respect and safety, of being valued and heard.
PSYCHO-LOGICAL ABUSE	Inconsistency, incompleteness, being hard to read, not telling the "whole story", not taking "no" for an answer	Leaving the other person in a "one down" position because they can't read you, don't know where you stand, can't predict what you will do next. "Crazy making", changing your story. Violating NCO	Bait and switch strategies, lying, manipulation, inconsistencies, "crazy making" to the point of making the other person doubt their sanity, stalking, property damage	Being consistent, predictable and reliable, telling the whole truth. Not using any manipulation or trickery even when you could get away with it.

MINIMIZA-TION, DENIAL AND BLAME	Brushing off the effect you have on the other person, not acknowledging the wrongness of what you have done, or the damage you have done	Openly denying that you did something, lying and deceiving, minimizing the effect it had, blaming it on the other person or something else.	Boldly blaming what you did or it's effects on the other person, denying that it happened, denying responsibility for what you did	Honesty and openness about what you did, honestly admitting to the damage it caused and making sincere amends to repair the damage when possible. Absence of blame.
USE OF FEAR, INTIMIDATION, COERCION AND THREATS	Doing things that frighten or intimidate, subtle implication of threat, use of coercion such as "if you do this you'll get that".	Openly using threats and fear to get your way or control the other person. Making them feel unsafe and having to "walk on eggshells". Threats to friends, pets, property	Threats that are carried out, no longer any negotiations on a level playing field, the other person no longer has a reasonable, free voice in what they say and do. Property damage, abuse of pets, threats to friends or family.	Create an environment of trust and safety in which choices are made freely and there is no issue of coercion.
SOCIAL ABUSE, ISOLATION	Censoring or passing judgment on what the other person can do, where they can go, who they should or can see, talk to, associate with, etc. Pulling away from them emotionally, not being emotionally available.	Open efforts to control or monitor their activities, phone calls, what they read, who they associate with. Interfering with friendships, activities or associations. Stalking.	The other person is a virtual prisoner. One or more friends, family or activities has been deemed unacceptable or unavailable. Threats to friends or family.	Open support and encouragement of all of their friendships, family relationships and activities. They feel safe, valued and supported.
FINANCIAL ABUSE WAC 388-60-0235 (10)	Failing to respond to reasonable expectations about what you will earn, how you will handle the money. Not giving the other person equal access to money, resources, and information about those things.	Openly not providing reasonable financial support, openly restricting access to money or information about money, where it is, what you are doing with it etc. Damage to personal property	Handling money and financial resources in such a way as to cause damage to the family or to the other person, cutting the person off from resources, mishandling the resources, openly cutting them off from resources and information. Financial ruin for them.	Sharing in all financial decisions in an equal way, sharing decision making and information and living up to reasonable financial and material expectations.
USING CHILDREN	Playing the children off against the other parent, making negative comments about the other parents. Using harsh physical, verbal or emotional punishments with the children.	Use of physical punishment, talking badly about the other parent, lobbying the children to take your side against the other parent, not sharing in parenting responsibilities	Reducing the children to being bargaining chips, expecting the children to take sides, manipulating visitations, using visitations to verbally abuse the other parent.	Sharing parenting in an open, responsible way, supporting the other parent.

RELATIONSHIP AMONG THE DIFFERENT FORMS OF VIOLENCE AND THEIR ORIGINS IN OUR PERSONAL AND SOCIAL INADEQUACIES

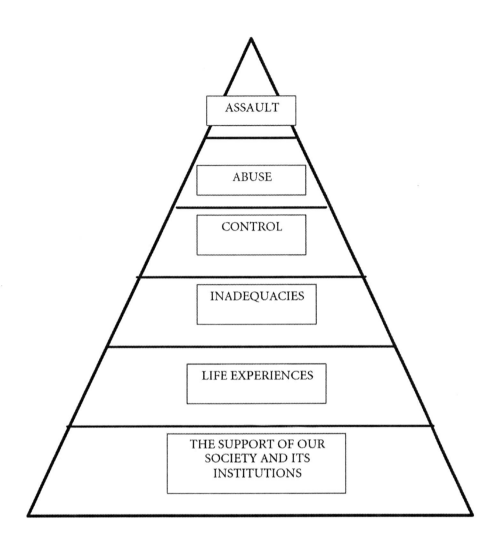

PATTERNS OF CONTROL, ABUSE, AND VIOLENCE

Periodically quitting drinking is part of continuing to drink.
Periodically quitting smoking is part of continuing to smoke.
Periodically going on a diet is part of continuing to over eat.
Periods of non-violence, of not being abusive or controlling, is part of the pattern of abuse, violence and control.
Sometimes, being good is part of getting ready to be bad again.

Violence doesn't occur constantly. Violence, since it is a small part of a larger pattern of abuse and control, usually occurs occasionally, and often as a part of a pattern of other behaviors. Often this pattern of behaviors creates the impression, or the illusion, that the violence has gone away. This is important to remember so that we don't fall into the trap of thinking that the violence has gone away, or is a one time only event, when in fact it is part of a pattern in which the violence can reoccur.

There are several patterns which account for most violence;

1. Violence which is cyclical
2. Violence which is intermittent
3. Violence which is affective.
4. Violence which is instrumental

Cyclical violence

One of the earliest patterns of violence was discussed by Lenore Walker. She discovered that most domestic violence occurred in a three phase pattern;
1. A period of overt use of anger and violence called the <u>Explosive Phase</u>.
2. Then the abuser would be ashamed of what they had done or become fearful of consequences and become contrite and apologetic, often trying to buy the forgiveness of the victim. This has often been called the <u>Honeymoon Phase</u>, but this is a poor choice of names. It's not a honeymoon for the recipient because they know that more abuse is on the way. Many victims of domestic violence have referred to this as the phenomena in which "being nice is the first step toward getting mean again." Although the offender may not be physically abusive there is usually a lot of psychological abuse, minimization and denial, and financial or emotional manipulation to force the victim into the position of not being able to hold the offender accountable.
3. The Honeymoon Phase can last hours, days, months or years. But inevitably, if the underlying issues aren't addressed, the next phase is the <u>Tension Building Phase</u>. As the name implies, this is a time when the offender begins to feel victimized, put upon, depressed or angry. Tension begins to build and arguments start to escalate. Eventually the arguments become worse and finally erupt in the Explosive Phase again.

Because there are so many ways to be controlling, abusive or violent, and because we can use different forms of control, abuse or violence each time around the cycle, we can convince ourselves that there is no pattern. We can convince ourselves that we are trying something different each time, when, in fact, we are just doing different versions of the same thing over and over again. We are trapped in the cycle of violence by our denial that we are being controlling, abusive or violence. We are trapped in a cycle by denying that we are in a cycle.

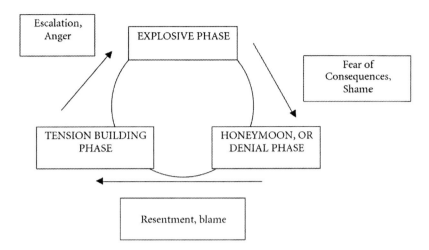

Intermittent control, abuse, or violence

It would be difficult to be controlling, abusive or violent all the time. Another pattern of violence is Intermittent Violence. Why do gamblers gamble, even when they only win some of the time? Why did Southwester Native Americans believe that rain dancing worked, when it only worked sometimes? Why do any of us persist in patterns of behavior which only work sometimes?

The answer is that the type of learning which is the hardest to break or unlearn is called "partial reinforcement" or "intermittent reinforcement". What this means is that we can actually train ourselves–and others–in a pattern of behavior in which failure is part of success.

1. When gambling, losing is part of winning, because it seems that the longer you lose, the closer you come to winning.
2. If you dance long enough, it will eventually rain, so you think that the dance you are doing at that particular moment is the one that led to the rain.
3. If any system of learning or behavior gets results only now and then, we will persist in that behavior even if it isn't rewarded any more.

The same thing happens when something happens to me randomly. If I ask you to pass the salt thousands of times and you pass the salt, then one day when I ask you to pass the salt you yell at me and scare me and call me horrible names, I'll remember that. Then you apologize to me and for another thousand times when I ask you to pass the salt you just pass the salt. Eventually I'll relax and no longer be afraid to ask you to pass the salt. Then one day I ask you to pass the salt and you blow up and throw the eggs on me. Your position is that you have only gotten angry at me twice for asking you to pass the salt, that it was years apart. However, no matter what the logic is that you use, the fact is that being nice thousands of times doesn't reduce the chances that you will yell at me.

When control, abuse, or violence is only intermittent, only sometimes, it has the added effect that not only do you reserve the right to use control, abuse, or violent, but also that if you are good that might only mean that being good is part of being abusive. It also means that there really isn't any way that I can predict or expect your behavior. I need to always be on my guard.

This is why reducing controlling, abusive, or violent behavior isn't worth much. If you want someone to be able to love and trust you, you have to stop it completely. Only stopping it sometimes, even if you only relapse occasionally, means that you are still likely to do it again, eventually.

Affective Control, Abuse or Violence

This is the pattern of control, abuse or violence which is the most commonly talked about. This means that I become controlling, abusive or violent if I get depressed enough, frustrated enough, drunk enough, or angry enough. In this pattern of control, abuse and violence the other person is safe only as long as I am happy and getting my way. If I feel good, then I act good. I am "normal" during those times. But, if for whatever reason, I feel bad, then I reserve the right to blow up at you. I might defend my behavior as being blamed on a bad temper, on being "stressed out" or "at the end of my rope". I could blame it on you, for example, telling you that "you shouldn't push my buttons when I'm feeling this way".

But the bottom line is that this is a very clear cut way of me controlling you. If I'm unhappy, you could get physically or emotionally hurt or you could simply have to put up with a disgusting display of self pity on my part. But you *will* pay. You don't know when, you don't know how. But you will pay if you don't make sure that I am happy and getting my way.

Instrumental control, abuse, or violence

This means simply that I use control, abuse, or violence because it gets me what I want. I yell at you so that eventually you will give in. I take money out of your purse because I want the money. I demand sex because I want sex. I ignore your sexual needs because it's easier than being a good lover.

I do it because I want to and because it works.

The sneaky thing about this form of control, abuse, or violence is that I don't have to do it very often to get you to be obedient or compliant with me. Sometimes only once per relationship. But the memory persists; I am going to win eventually, no matter what. You are going to lose eventually, no matter what.

Consequently sometimes a person can be violent only once, early in a relationship, to establish that they will use whatever force necessary to get their way, and the recipient will remember that and be controlled by fear of that behavior for decades.

Why this is important to note is that many people, as part of their denial, will feel that just because they haven't done anything overtly violent for years that this isn't a domestic violence relationship. In fact, as long as the other person fears consequences if I feel bad, then I am consciously or unconsciously getting my way through fear. And that is violence.

2. THE BELIEFS AND VALUES WHICH SUPPORT CONTROL, ABUSE, OR VIOLENCE

WAC 388-60-0245 (1), (2)

Every time Charlie went to a particular warehouse he was greeted by a very attractive, seductive woman who seemed attracted to him. Eventually he asked the manager of the warehouse what her name was so he could ask her out.

"Well," sighed the manager, "the name is Betty, but that isn't a woman."

Horrified, Charlie avoided the cross dresser every time he went there until he/she gave up.

Years later he was at that warehouse again, and there was a new manager.

"What ever happened to that cross-dresser Betty?" he asked.

The new manager laughed and laughed.

"That was no cross-dresser. That was the manager's daughter. He just told guys like you that story to keep you from messing with her."

We respond to what we think, not to what really is there. The reality is that we have control over what we do with our hands, feet, and mouths, but as long we believe that other people, circumstances, the past, or whatever can control us, we don't believe that we have control over ourselves. Not because we don't, but because we think we don't.

Go back to the first section about anger management and look over the part about rational and irrational thinking.

One part of learning how to control ourselves is to learn how to look at the beliefs, values and self talk we use which leads to our misbehavior. Our reaction to anything is not controlled by what happened, but by how and what we think about it. What were you thinking at the time? What were you telling yourself?

For example, whether I am happy or unhappy with the trade in value I get for my car depends upon what I think the "right" price is. If I get more than I expect, I'm happy. If I get less, then I am unhappy. Let's say I get more than what I expect, and I'm happy, then, later, if I find out it was actually a rare, collectable car worth ten times as much, I'm unhappy. Then, if still later I learn I was lied to, that I really got twice what it was worth, I'm happy again.

In reality, the amount of money I got for the car hasn't changed, even though my mood changed twice. Only my self talk, my thoughts, my beliefs changed.

In the same way we evaluate and interpret everything that happens to us. The result of that evaluation, that self talk, is what causes our reactions. To control our reactions, we have to control our thoughts. When we are in control of our thoughts, we don't need control over anything else.

If we don't like the results we are getting in our relationships, on our jobs, or just in how we feel about ourselves and our lives, the answer doesn't like in the world. It's just a world. It does what worlds do. It's just a matter of cause and effect. The answer lies in how effectively we respond to the world, how well we handle things. And that depends on how clearly and rationally we perceive the situation; how rationally and clearly we think.

We get what we get, because we do what we do. To get something different, we have to do something different. We do what we do because we think what we think. If we want to do something different, we have to think something different. And, to understand that, we have to learn how to look at the accuracy and the rationality of our thoughts and feelings.

An irrational belief isn't necessarily wrong, so much as it has been taken too far. For example, we don't have to like paying taxes, but it's irrational to think that we can't stand it. We don't have to like going to work, but it's irrational to think it's terrible and unfair.

So the old expression "What were you thinking?" is actually not just being argumentative. When you know what you were thinking, you have control over your life.

Examples of irrational beliefs	Result of that belief in our feelings and behavior	Examples of rational counter beliefs	Result of the rational counter in our feelings and behavior
"I must be loved by the people I love"	An urgent need to get the people I love to love me no matter what; disastrous feelings if they don't	"I'd really, really, *really* like the people I love to love me, but they have free will and I have to accept it if they don't, even if it makes me sad"	Less urgent relationships in which people are free to love me and don't feel urgent or pressured about it. Also, I'll pick relationships with people who really do like me
"I can't stand it if people disagree with me."	Unnecessary distress if people have different opinions or ideas than you do, desire to control their opinions, conflicts and fights result	"I like it better when people agree with me, but I know what I think, and I don't need their agreement for me to feel good."	Fewer conflicts, less anger, better relationships.
"If someone respects you, they won't do things that make you unhappy."	Lots of disappointments in love and other relationships, unnecessary distress over what loved ones do, and endless fights over "If you really loved me you would do …"	"I like it when you do things that make me happy, but just because someone loves me, doesn't mean that they will always do what I want them to do. I don't have a right to expect that of you."	Better relationships, less conflict, more negotiation.
"I deserve better than what I'm getting."	Anger, bitterness, resentment, emotional withdrawal, blameful thinking.	"Everyone deserves the very best, but that doesn't necessarily mean that they will get it just because they deserve it. I want a lot more out of life, but it's up to me to do what it takes to get it."	Better problem solving, better relationship, fewer emotional problems, more success, better life.
"I can't stand being alone, I have to be in a relationship or life is unbearable."	Urgent, desperate relationships, often inappropriate, just to avoid being alone.	"I really like being in a relationship but I like my own company, too, and I don't have to compromise just to be in a relationship."	Better relationships, less self doubt, less shame, fewer fights. Quality over quantity.

Hurting or controlling someone you love is basically an irrational activity. In reality it makes absolutely no sense to yell at someone you hope will love you, or trick someone you hope will trust you. It makes no sense, so there must be an irrational belief leading us to those actions.

Somehow, we have to be indulging in some sort of irrational thinking in order to come up with irrational behavior. If we are to make sense out of hurting or scaring someone we love, we must distort our thinking. Otherwise it would make no sense.

To get control over our lives we have to get control over what we do, and to do that, we need to get control over our thinking.

Ideas about power

There are two kinds of power.

The first is power over ourselves. Most religions, psychologies, and philosophies tell us that the only true power is power over ourselves. Self control. True power is not over other people. Only a weak person wants control over someone else. A strong person has no need to control other people. Wanting to have control over other people is a sign of weakness.

True power is based upon self-respect, maturity, and true competence. Not control over other people. If you respect yourself and have control over yourself and your actions, there is nothing anyone can do to control you or change how you feel. Nothing.

The other kind of power is power over other people. This inevitably requires that we have some sort of fear, force, or advantage in order to get other people to do what we want, in order to have power over the other person. Our society is based upon this kind of power over other people. People who have power are seen as leaders, heroes, or role models. Often they are rewarded for successfully using power over other people.

This kind of power is inevitably based upon fear. People who want this sort of power are frightened people. Weak people. If they weren't weak, they wouldn't be trying to get more and more power over other people. They fear that if they don't have power over other people, whether that is another race, another nation, another group of people, another gang, or our spouses or children, that they will be rejected or hurt in some way. That they have to have power over other people to feel good about themselves, or safe.

People who aren't afraid, who genuinely have something to offer the world or their family, don't want the second kind of power, because it will inevitably fail; anything based upon power, fear or force will collapse because people don't like being controlled that way.

Examples of beliefs about power include, but aren't limited to;
- Might makes rights
- The best defense is a good offense
- Good guys finish last
- A ship can only have one captain
- Too many cooks spoil the stew
- Winning isn't just the most important thing: it's the *only* thing
- Sharing is for sissies
- Compromise is another form of losing
- Winning is a sign that I am right.
- To be a winner I have to make someone else lose.
- I am weak if I don't have power over other people.

Ideas about gender and family

Our society also has a lot of ideas about gender, family and the power and about the control a man can or should have over his family. For many centuries women and children simply had no rights. These beliefs also came from times and places where it was okay to rape, torture, kill and own people of different races, religions, sexes, or lower socioeconomic classes. This sort of thinking led to the laws and traditions that made women, families, and people of other races or economic groups simply possessions to be used and discarded. Now that we have learned how to use indoor plumbing, eat with a fork, and drive cars, we need to grow up and leave those antiquated ideas behind.

Some of the beliefs our society has taught us about power and control in families;

- A man should be the head of the household
- Men are more naturally leaders than women are
- Women should take care of men
- Women are more able to take care of things at home than men are
- House work is "just house work"
- Men are more able to take care of things outside the home than women are
- Work outside the home is more important than work in the home
- Logic is more important than emotions when it comes to making decisions
- Somebody has to make the decisions
- The person who "brings home the bacon" has a right to dominate the home
- A man has the right to punish family members who are disobedient to him
- The man's ability to "keep order in his family" is more important than the rights of the individuals involved
- Keeping the family intact is more important than the rights, needs, feelings and even the safety of the individuals involved
- A woman doesn't have the right to leave a family she has a commitment to, even if the man violates that commitment by being controlling, abusive or violent
- A man has different rights over someone with whom they are in a family relationship or sexual relationship than they would with strangers
- Women and children need to know their place
- We are more respected if we put people in their place through fear and force
- If we don't put them in their place through fear and force, they won't respect us.
- Having control over the people in your relationships is a sign of strength

Beliefs about provocation

Because we can use ideas about provocation to justify the use of force, we use those beliefs a lot. We used them to justify killing off the Native Americans, invading any number of countries, lynching African Americans, colonizing countries that didn't really need to be colonized, and all the world wars. Rapists often justify their rapes by claiming to be provoked by women who were dressed or were acting "provocatively." The whole idea of "walking around with a chip on your shoulder" is to get someone to do something that you can use to justify a fight as being "provoked" by his or her reaction.

Thus we can justify controlling other people, instead of controlling ourselves, by reasoning that if we can get the other person to do what we want them to do, we can control our anger at them: we control ourselves by controlling them. All they have to do to prevent getting controlled, abused, or violated is to do what we want them to do. And that, specifically, includes not "provoking me". And that means I'm controlling them out of fear.

In fact, there is no such thing as provocation other than the provocation we justify in our thinking. Obviously, if something provokes one person but not another, the "provocation" lies in the mind of the provoked person. What provokes one person won't provoke another person. What provokes me at one time won't provoke me at another. In other words, there is no such thing as provocation.

I went to college in Walla Walla, Washington, in the late 60's and early 70's, a time of great unrest, especially regarding the Viet Nam war. Walla Walla was notoriously conservative at that time. As part of an experiment for one of our classes, we had a drama student present a speech against the war to a local union meeting. The participants were asked to not discuss the speech or their reactions to it during the speech. One third of them were given feedback sheets which described the speech as being part of his grade for speech class and that the subject had been randomly chosen and did not reflect his actual beliefs. The second third got the same scoring sheet, but it indicated that the speaker was a conscientious objector to the war and the speech was part of his obligation in order to not get drafted, and the speech reflected his real beliefs. The last third were given the same rating sheet, but were told he was a drama student delivering a humorous parody of "antiwar objectors" and this was part of his grade in comedy class.

They were all asked to rate the speech according to a number of scales, including how much they "liked" the speech and how much they "liked" the speaker.

The third who were told that this was a comical parody were greatly entertained and liked both the speaker and the speech. The third who thought it was just a randomly chosen speech found it dry and somewhat uninteresting. The third who were told it was his sincere beliefs could barely contain themselves from jumping out of their chairs and assaulting him.

Same speech. Three different reactions based upon the intentions they projected upon the speaker. So did the speech provoke the last third, or did their beliefs provoke them?

Beliefs and values we can indulge in which support the myth of "provocation":

- Another person's actions can control what we do
- Our reactions, if we can find a way to feel provoked, are the fault of the other person, not us
- We aren't responsible for what we do if we feel provoked
- We are justified in controlling other people to keep them from making us angry
- Some people must simply want to fight, otherwise, why would they provoke one?
- Provoking a fight, argument, or conflict means it's okay for us to respond violently
- Some actions on the part of other people justify or warrant a violent or controlling response

3. THE EFFECTS OF CONTROL, ABUSE AND VIOLENCE

WAC 388-60-0245 (5)

To really get a handle on changing controlling, abusive, or violent behavior we have to understand the consequences of what we are doing.

Family violence is destroying American families.

And it doesn't have to be this way. Forty percent of all marriages end in divorce, and in about one quarter of those divorces, domestic violence is cited as the cause of the divorce. In other words, ten percent of all marriages in the United States will end because of needless, pointless, unnecessary violence. That also means that ten percent or more of the children from broken homes are growing up in broken homes because of domestic violence. Estimates are that up to half of the homeless women and children in the United States are homeless because they are escaping from domestic violence. Up to half of all police calls in the United States are for domestic violence cases.

Everyone loses.

The pressure to force families to stay together in spite of family violence is well intended, but misbegotten. People should not be forced to stay in a violent situation. It doesn't help the children to grow up seeing this as the way men and women should relate. It doesn't help the abusive person to enable them to progress further and further down the path of control, abuse and ultimately violent. Home is not–or at least should not–be a prison. A marriage should not be a life sentence, without parole.

That isn't a home. Control, abuse, and/or violence aren't home life.

It makes no sense. Love and fear cannot coexist. Our brains aren't built that way. To prevent the families from being destroyed we need to stop the violence, to prevent it from even beginning.

If we can begin to understand the effects–sometimes lasting years–of a single act of anger, a single cruel word, we would live so much more carefully.

Effects on Children of Witnessing Family Violence.

- 50% of the men who frequently assaulted their wives also frequently abused their children.
- Children witnessing the violence inflicted on their mothers evidence behavioral, physical, or emotional problems similar to those experienced by physically abused children
- These children have a six times greater chance of committing suicide, 24 percent greater chance committing sexual assault crimes and a 50 percent greater likelihood of abusing drugs and alcohol
- Boys become aggressive, fighting with siblings and schoolmates and having temper tantrums. Girls are more likely to become passive, clinging, and withdrawn
- Male children who witness the abuse of mothers by fathers are more likely to become men who batter in adulthood than those male children from homes free of violence
- More than half of the young men between the ages of 11 and 22 who are in jail for homicide have killed their mother's batterer.
- Child witnesses of domestic violence to exhibit more aggressive and antisocial (often called "externalized" behaviors) as well as fearful and inhibited behaviors ("internalized" behaviors), and to show lower social competence than other children.
- Children who witnessed violence were also found to show more anxiety, self-esteem, depression, anger, and temperament problems than children who did not witness violence at home.
- Children from homes where their mothers were being abused have shown less skill in understanding how others feel and examining situations from others' perspectives when compared to children from non-violent households. Peer relationships, autonomy, self-control, and overall competence were also reported significantly lower among boys who had experienced serious physical violence and been exposed to the use of weapons between adults living in their homes.
- Increased violence exposure associated with lower cognitive functioning
- Witnessing violence as a child was associated with adult reports of depression, trauma-related symptoms, and low self-esteem among women and trauma-related symptoms alone among men.

There is a wider range of effects on our partners but they are all negative and they all push our loved ones away.

Effects on victims or recipients of domestic violence, abuse, or control

- Physical abuse is the single leading cause of women seeking medical attention in emergency rooms.
- Women in abusive relationships have frequent headaches, chronic generalized pain, and pelvic pain, frequent vaginal and urinary tract infections, gastrointestinal (stomach and intestine) problems and eating disorders.
- Women in abusive relationships have more physical symptoms related to stress, anxiety disorders or depression.
- Physical abuse is one of the leading causes of death in young women.
- Physical abuse is one of the leading causes of miscarriages in pregnant women.
- Emotional and physical abuse is one of the leading causes of suicide attempts and successful suicides among women.
- Victims of domestic violence may be isolated from friends, family and neighbors and lose their network of social support.
- Divorce or being single due to domestic violence is one of the leading causes of poverty among women and the leading cause of children being raised in single parent families and/or in poverty.
- Being in abusive or controlling relationships causes low self esteem, occupational problems and emotional problems.

- Post Traumatic Stress Disorder (PTSD) is the most common diagnosis for women who have survived controlling, abusive or violent relationship with symptoms similar to being in a war, being a prisoner, or similar to the results of being kidnapped or raped.

How this destroys our families

A home is supposed to be a happy place. A place we go to feel safe and warm and loved. Anything less than that, whatever other imperfections a home may have, is not what a home or family or relationship should be.

The most obvious way that family violence destroys our families is that our families can't stay with us if we are controlling, abusive or violent. If you push people away hard enough, they leave. It's that simple. The more we try to force them to stay, force them to be obedient, force them to make the appearance of a family, the more we are forcing them to leave. If not physically, at least emotionally.

Love and fear can't exist in the same place at the same time. Fear pushes out the love. Eventually, there is no love, only fear.

Do you really want someone to stay with you just because they are afraid to leave you? Wouldn't you rather have them stay with you because they loved and trusted you?

Human beings have an inherent desire to feel good about themselves, to have self respect, to even take pride in themselves. To feel that they have some sort of control over their lives and circumstances. The more they feel like they are being controlled, the less free will they have, the more dragged down they are by negative comments or behavior, the less able they are to satisfy the basic instinct to want to feel good.

People can't feel good about themselves if they are being controlled. It runs contrary to human nature. To the degree that you attempt to control or dominate another person, they can't be with you.

It really is that simple.

They may not leave you physically. They may just tune you out. They may stop caring. They may stop trying. They will certainly leave you emotionally, mentally and spiritually. Do you really want someone to stay with you because you coerced them to? Do you really want someone to stay with you because you convinced them no one else would have them? Do you really want someone to stay with you because you convinced them they didn't deserve better?

They may resort to drugs, alcohol, promiscuity, gambling, spending, compulsive exercising, religion, or hobbies to make up for what they aren't getting from you. They might have affairs or just look elsewhere for their love and attention or safety. Or, if they don't find some other way to feel safe they could become depressed, mentally ill, or even kill themselves. Children often run away from home, become truant, or develop emotional or mental problems. Teenagers with drug or alcohol, problems, unplanned pregnancies, child prostitutes are usually the victims of family violence in their homes.

When you do the following exercises you will be expected to identify the results of what you have done in each category, the effects on the recipient. There may be other effects not listed on this handout, so become a good detective and find out what the specific effects have been in your particular case.

For each effect you have had on those you love you are expected to identify, and perform, the amends for that action.

4. OUR INADEQUACIES

Life isn't long enough for all of us to become competent in everything we need to know. Life is a process of constantly having to learn from our mistakes so that we become more competent and move on. There is no shame in making mistakes, as long as we learn from them and change how we do thing so that we don't make those mistakes anymore.

Life is not easy enough that all of us can make it through life without some scars, some psychological or emotional injuries, which leave us less able to do what we need to do. Life is a process of identifying those psychological problems, fixing them, and moving on.

Control, abuse, and violence are *always* the least effective ways to address any problem, meet any need, or communicate any feeling. Control, abuse or violence is *always* the most sincere way of admitting that you are incompetent, in some way, on that subject. Admitting that you lack a skill, or have an emotional or psychological problem.

- If I steal money, it's an admission that I don't have the job skills to earn it. That would be my inadequacy. It's not someone else's fault that I don't have that skill.
- If I yell at someone it's an admission that I don't have the verbal skills to say it correctly. That's my inadequacy. It's not someone else's fault that I don't have that skill.
- If I have to use force to get my spouse to do what I want, it's an admission that I'm not a good enough partner for her to want to work together with me, or that what I'm asking for is inappropriate. That's my inadequacy. It's not her fault that I don't know how to be a good enough partner.

Consequently, each form of abuse that we use, each time that we use it, is an admission that in that way, we are inadequate, some lack of skill, some emotional or psychological problem in that area. There's no shame in that. In each of the following assignments there is a section for you to identify what the inadequacy is that led you to that inappropriate behavior and what you need to do to fix it.

We need to not only stop our control, abuse or violence and replace it with more appropriate responses, we need to find out what the inadequacies were which motivated us to do something ineffective and inappropriate and address those inadequacies.

- If you used emotional abuse to hurt your partner's feelings to avoid intimacy, then perhaps the inadequacy is that you fear intimacy. The cure could be that you would need to spend more time with your partner, sharing your feelings and baring your soul so that you can face those fears and become a stronger, better person.
- If you are financially controlling and blame your financial problems on your partner perhaps the real issue is that you don't know how to handle money. A possible solution would be to go to Consumer Credit Counseling or a similar agency, or even a private accountant, to help you learn how to handle your money better.
- If you are jealous and possessive of your partner and resent their outside friendships, relationships or activities, perhaps your inadequacy is low self esteem ("I'm not a good enough partner for her to want to stick around") or some other insecurity. Perhaps it would be good to address those feelings in your group, or perhaps in individual therapy.

Part of each of the following assignments is to identify what your inadequacies were for each time you did something controlling, abusive, or violent, what you need to do to address that inadequacy, and making a commitment to address that inadequacy. Until we address the inadequacy which motivated us to use control, abuse or violence, the risk of it occurring again could still be there.

5. WHAT WE COULD HAVE OR SHOULD HAVE DONE DIFFERENTLY

Refer back to the fourth column on page 57. There is always an alternative to control, abuse, or violence. For each of the assignments, refer back to this list and look at what you could have, or should have, done differently. Be creative. There are more non-abusive, non-controlling alternatives than there are wrong ways to do things. What specifically would have been more appropriate?

How do we change our behavior? This is a time-honored question. However, the reality is that we are all changing our behavior every day.

All change begins and ends with our thinking. We change when we think correctly about things. We can change in a fluid, adaptive manner when we have the right attitude about change.

The following are nine "thinking steps" which I find very useful to help myself and other people to have the right attitude toward change in order to learn how to change their behavior in a comfortable, effective manner.

1. We have control over what we do with our hands, feet, and mouths.

This is an important place to start. Do you think we have control over what we do with our hands, feet, and mouths? Most people would agree. But what about the case that we don't have *perfect* control over what we do with our hands, feet, or mouths? A diamond cutter, professional golfer, award-winning dancer, or professional speaker could do things with their hands, feet, or mouths better than I could. They have had more practice than I have. But with practice I could be better.

So I don't have *perfect* control over my hands, feet and mouth. But I still have control over what I do with them.

There is also the situation of the epileptic who doesn't have perfect control over his or her hands or feet. But they can take medications to reduce the frequency and intensity of the unwanted movements of their hands, feet, and mouth. They can follow therapeutic diets and lifestyles. So, again, while they can't categorically change what their hands and feet and mouths do, they have some control over it.

Someone who is blind drunk may not have control over their hands, feet, mouth, and/or bladder. But they can stop drinking, and thus regain control. The best way to control what we do when drunk is to not drink.

In fact, all of us have direct or indirect control over everything that we do with our hands, feet and mouths.

Can you accept this? If not, don't proceed until you have had a chance to struggle with this issue and see if you can find any exceptions to it, direct or indirect.

2. What we do with our hands, feet and mouths has a goal, motive, purpose, intention, purpose or function.

In other words, nothing we do is meaningless. Can you think of anything you do which is meaningless? Even scratching or yawning has a purpose. We stretch to relieve muscle tension and we yawn to get more oxygen. We get out of bed because we want to get up; we go to bed because we are tired. If we get up and go back to bed it's because we want to sleep more than we want to get up.

If even such small behaviors have a goal or purpose or function, then so does everything else we do in life. Even our mistakes are made for a reason. We choose the wrong career or partner because it is convenient, we didn't want to plan any more, or some such reason. Even what we *don't* do has a goal, motive, purpose or intention. Such as not going to work, or not planning.

Can you accept this? Don't go on to the next point until you have grappled with each exception, and found the goal or purpose behind everything we do with our hands, feet or mouths.

3. If so, then everything we do is a chosen tactic or means to an end toward meeting those goals, needs, purposes, functions or whatever.

This is a hard one to debate because if we accept that we have control over what we do with our hands, feet, and mouths and that what we do with our hands, feet and mouths is somehow, at some level, purposeful, then it would follow that what we do is a chosen means to an end. We do it because there is something that we want. What we do might not be successful. But the purpose is there. We might not even know why, but we could figure it out later and realize that yes, there was a purpose to what we did and what we did was a means to that end.

4. If we can choose one thing to achieve that goal, purpose or function, we could also have chosen to do something else, something different.

There are seven routes I can take from home to work. Some are shorter, some are longer. It is always a guess which route will get me to work the fastest. Some days I'm right about which one is the fastest. Sometimes I'm wrong. I might have the best reasons in the world for which one I chose and still be wrong. I could always have chosen a different route.

Consequently, the route I choose, and the result in terms of how long it takes, are my responsibility. Not anyone else's.

There are some cases where you would be really, really stupid to make a different choice, such as taking, or not taking, the money you just won at the lottery, or jumping out of the way of speeding car. But you still could have made the different choice. It's important to remember that.

I could have chosen the person I'm with for a partner, or not. I could have chosen someone else, or I could have chosen to be alone. The choice is mine. I'm in the relationship voluntarily.

When in doubt, we can always choose to do nothing. There could be a price we pay, but the choice is ours. We are voluntarily choosing the price we want to pay.

5. Thus I can't blame my choices, or their results, on other people or circumstances.

If I choose one particular route to work, and end up getting caught in a traffic jam, I have no one to blame. I chose to be there. I didn't choose the traffic jam. I had no control over that. But I was there by choice. If I take the money from the lottery and it ends up ruining my life, it was my choice. I can't blame the lottery commission. If I live on Big Macs and get fat, it isn't McDonald's fault. If I jump left instead of right when the car is coming at me, and end up in the blackberry bushes, it's the fault of the driver that they drove at me, but landing in the sticker bushes instead of the lawn was my call.

In the same fashion we can't blame our decision to use fear or force, our decision to control, abuse, or violate another person, or the results of that decision, on other people or circumstances. If nothing else, we could always have chosen to just do nothing. The choice was ours, we made our choice, the results are the results of our choices.

6. You can't change other people. You can only change the things you do, to which they respond.

If someone doesn't trust me, then I haven't done what it takes for them to trust me. I may or may not want to do what it takes, but they sure as heck won't trust me until I do what it takes for them to trust me.

If someone doesn't love me, it's because I haven't done what it takes for them to love me. If it is something simple, like using more deodorant, then I may choose to do what it takes. If it's something more, like giving them all my money, then I may or may not choose to do it. The choice is mine. If it means compromising my moral or ethical values, then I probably won't choose to do it. And if, as a result of my choice, they choose to not be with me, then it isn't their fault that I chose to not become an astronaut. It was my call.

In any case, I can't change the other person's mind. All I can change is what I am doing to which they are responding, if I so choose. Or not. If we try to change other people, to force them to respond or behave or react differently to me, then I will end up trapped in a pattern of control, and eventually violence. If, instead, I take control over myself, over what I do, then I will have control over my life without power and control, without fear or force, without abuse.

7. You *get* what you *get* because you *do* what you *do*. If you want to *get* something different, you have to *do* something different.

This is really hard to disagree with, because it is so true. If I want different results, I have to change what I do. They say that insanity is doing the same thing over and over again and expecting different results. I couldn't agree more.

8. You *do* what you *do* because you *think* what you *think*. If you want to *do* something different, you have to *think* something different.

Education is about changing what we think. Teaching us to add and subtract is changing how we think. Learning to not put our hands on a hot stove is learning.

Life experience is about changing what and how we think. With experience and maturity we have better skills, more information. We can make better choices and thus do different things. If I think a snake is poisonous, I'll be afraid of it. If I learn that it isn't, I won't be afraid of it. If I have an irrational fear of snakes, I can learn different beliefs about snakes and give myself different experiences with snakes and overcome the fear.

This is not just what the section about irrational beliefs is about. This is what the whole program is about. In fact, this is what all of life is about. Learning from our experiences and changing our minds to get different results.

The only thing that can make our lives better or worse is how quickly we learn from our experiences and adapt what and how we think.

9. The only thing you *can* change in life is what you think, and the only thing you *need* to change in life is how you think.

This exercise, this book, this program, and this life is about changing what you think, so that you can change what you do, so that you can change what you get, and have a happier life.

As you go through the following exercises, in addition to identifying the abusive or controlling behaviors you have done, you will be expected to identify the irrational beliefs and values you used to justify your control, abuse and/or violence and what the truth is about that subject. The rational counter for those ideas and beliefs. What we need to learn to think and believe and feel so that we don't respond with control, abuse and violence. What you should have done and could have done different, better.

6. APOLOGY AND AMENDS

Control, abuse and violence cause damage. When we cause damage, whether it is physical, emotional, financial or social damage, we have to fix the damage we did.

To be a responsible person, we have to repair the damage we have done. If you aren't willing to repair the damage you have done, then you aren't really sorry and you aren't really being responsible.

It really is that simple. Even if you can't have contact with the other person, at the very least you have to responsibly figure out and admit what it is that you should do if you could.

There are two parts to properly making amends.

Apology

For an apology to count it has to be sincere. You have to really be sorry for what you did. In making your apologies in the following exercises you will need to;

- Be sincere. A flippant apology is another form of an insult. "Awright, I'm sorry, what's the big deal?" Instead, say "What I did was wrong, and I really apologize."
- Be complete. Don't just say "I'm sorry for all the bad things I did". Instead, be thorough. For example in the "Physical" part of the handouts, don't just say "I'm sorry I hurt you." Say "I'm sorry that on your birthday I pushed you away. I'm sorry that at Christmas I slammed the door on you. I'm sorry that I pushed you away when you wanted a hug."
- Explain why it was bad. "I'm sorry that I called your mother a slut. She isn't a slut, she doesn't deserve to be called names, and it hurt her feelings and your feelings."

Amends

Amends are what you do to repair the damage you did. For example, if you broke something, you have to replace it. If you took something, you have to return it. If you alienated her from friends and family, you need to do everything in your power to restore those relationships. If you did something that cost the other person money, you need to pay them back. If you lied in court about the other person, you need to go back to court to correct the lie.

For example if I told your friends that you were over reacting and had complained about my abuse just to get some advantage or call attention to yourself, I need to find each of those people and tell them that I lied, that I was abusive and you weren't making it up.

The amends have to be thorough and appropriate to what the damage was.

- If something I did or left undone cost you money, I need to repay you
- If something I did hurt you physically, I have to make your life physically better
- If I called you bad names—verbal abuse–I need to use words to make you feel better by honestly and sincerely only using positive statements with you.
- If I made you afraid I have to create an environment of safety and trust.
- If I minimized or denied anything that I did I have to completely and honestly tell you–and whoever else I told those things to—the truth, without minimization or denial.
- If I was confusing and sneaky, I have to be as open as a book.
- If I was crazy making, I need to be clear and predicable.

Remember, even if you can't actually do these things to repair the damage you did, you have to be honest and thorough in totaling up what you owe.

7. WHAT ARE THE APOLOGY AND AMENDS I HAVE DONE THIS WEEK? WHAT ARE THE NON-ABUSIVE, NON-CONTROLLING ALTERNATIVES I HAVE PRACTICED THIS WEEK?

The last part of each assignment is where the rubber meets the road; what have you done *this week* which makes amends; what have you done *this week* to practice the non-abusive, non-controlling alternatives to the abusive behavior?

If the abuse was being controlling, what have you done which empowered the other person, or someone else, if you aren't with that person? If you were stingy, what have you done this week which was generous? If the abuse was to use fear, what have you done which created safety?

Using the information in these sections you are now ready to move on to the next phase in the assignments. This is inventorying the specific forms of control, abuse and violence you have used.

ASSIGNMENT SEVEN
PHYSICAL ABUSE

What are the forms of physical abuse (unwanted touching or any other form of physical contact) that I have done both in the immediate situation, which brought me here, and in the entire relationship?
_____
_____

Why was that wrong? _____
_____
_____

What were the irrational thoughts or beliefs I used to justify what I did? _____
_____
_____

What would be more appropriate things to believe and think? _____
_____
_____

What was the damage or effect it had on the other person? _____
_____
_____

What could I have done that wouldn't have been controlling, abusive or violent?
_____
_____

What are my shortcomings or inadequacies which motivated me to do something abusive?
_____
_____

What do I need to do to fix those shortcomings or inadequacies, so that I don't do this again?
_____
_____

What should my apology be? _____
_____
_____

What should my amends be?
_____
_____

What are the apology, and amends I have done this week for this abuse?_____
_____

What are the non-controlling, non-abusive alternatives I have used this week (physical respect and comfort)?
_____
_____

Name_____ Submitted ___/___/___

ASSIGNMENT EIGHT
SEXUAL ABUSE AND ADVANTAGE

Who were the **people** who served as my role models for what sexuality between two people should be? _____
_____

What was their relationship like? _____
_____

What was the **message** I got from those people about what sexuality should be between two people? _____
_____

What were the **events or experiences** which shaped my experience of what sexuality between two people should be and are? _____
_____

What were the **attitudes** I learned from those events or experiences? _____
_____

What effects did those attitudes and experiences have on my later intimate relationships? _____
_____

What have I learned from the **media** about sexuality between two people? _____
_____

What have I learned from the media about female sexuality? _____
_____

What have I learned from the media about male sexuality? _____
_____

What did I learn about the role emotions play in sexuality for men? _____
_____

What did I learn about the role emotions play in sexuality for women? _____
_____

Have I ever been lied to about sex or been lied to so that someone else could get sex?
_____
_____

How did it make me feel? _____
_____

Have I ever lied to someone else about sex, or to get sex? _____
_____

How do I think it made that person feel? _____
_____

Has anyone ever disrespected my sexuality or my feelings in a sexual relationship?_____
_____

How did it make me feel? _____
_____

Have I ever disrespected another persons' feelings about sexuality or tenderness or romance? _____
_____

How do I think it made that person feel? _____
_____

Has anyone ever used me for sex in any way? _____
_____

How did it make me feel? _____
_____

Have I ever used someone for sex in some way? _____
_____

Have I ever gotten a woman pregnant who I wasn't prepared to marry, or at least support and help raise the child?
_____
_____

How do I think it made her feel? _____

_____

How do I think it made, or will make, the child feel? _____

_____

Has anyone been sexually unfaithful to me? _____

_____

How did it make me feel? _____

_____

Have ever been unfaithful to a sexual partner? _____

_____

How do I think it made that person feel? _____

_____

Have I ever used force, manipulation, or guilt to get someone to have sex with me? _____

_____

How do I think it made that person feel? _____

_____

Have I ever tricked anyone into being sexual or being sexual in a way she regretted later?____

_____

How do I think it made that person feel? _____

_____

Has anyone ever used my sexuality or sexual history against me or judged me sexually?____

_____

How did it make me feel? _____

_____

Have I ever used anyone's sexual history against them or judged them? _____
_____

How do I think it made that person feel? _____
_____

What would be the signs that my sexual behavior regarding the other person was having a negative effect on them?
_____
_____

Looking at all the things mentioned above, why were the things which I did which were sexually abusive or controlling wrong? _____
_____

What should I have done that would have been enhancing, not abusive or controlling? _____
_____

What was my motive for using abuse instead of respect and tenderness? _____
_____

What are my shortcomings or inadequacies which motivated me to do something abusive?
_____
_____

What do I need to do to fix those shortcomings or inadequacies so that I don't do this again? _____
_____

What were the irrational thoughts I used to justify my abusive behavior? _____
_____

What should I have thought or believed differently? _____
_____

What is the apology I owe? _____
_____

What are the amends I owe? _____
_____

What are the apology and amends I have made this week? _____
_____

What are the non-abusive, non-controlling alternatives or opposites to sexual abuse, which I have practiced this week(Sexual respect and intimacy, creating an atmosphere of comfort, dignity, and sexual fulfillment)? _____
_____
_____

Name_____ Submitted ___/___/___

ASSIGNMENT NINE
GENDER ABUSE

What are the forms of gender abuse that I have done both in the immediate situation, which brought me here, and in the entire relationship? How have I allowed or used issues of gender to control or abuse the other person (Indulging in personal, cultural, or religious stereotypes about gender and gender roles, taking advantage of gender differences, requiring, or expecting, that the other person should fulfill your gender expectations or fulfill tasks that you decide are gender specific, gender related jokes or cruelty, forcing the other person into roles or activities based upon your gender definition, belittling their gender, discrimination based upon their gender, making them gender prisoners or not being sensitive to their needs and feelings)? _____

_____

_____

In what ways was I not sensitive to their needs as being a person of their gender or gender orientation? _____

_____

In what ways did I treat them differently because they were in a sexual or gendered relationship with me which I wouldn't have done had they not been in a sexual or gendered relationship with me? _____

_____

Why was that wrong? _____

_____

What were the irrational thoughts I used to justify what I did? _____

_____

How should I change my beliefs and values so that I don't justify this sort of behavior in myself? _____

_____

What was the damage or effect it had on the other person? _____

_____

What could I have done that wouldn't have been controlling, abusive or violent? Which wouldn't have been discriminating toward the other person because of their gender?

_____

_____

What are my shortcomings or inadequacies which motivated me to do something abusive? _____

_____

What do I need to do to fix those shortcomings or inadequacies so that I don't do this again? _____
_____

What should my apology be? _____
_____

What should my amends be?_____
_____

What are the apology and amends I have done this week for this abuse? _____
_____

What are the non-abusive, non-controlling alternatives to gender abuse which I have practiced this week(Genuine equality of the sexes, respecting the rights, needs and feelings of all genders and gender orientations in an atmosphere of trust and safety)? _____
_____
_____

Name_____ Submitted ___/___/___

ASSIGNMENT TEN
EMOTIONAL ABUSE

What are the forms of emotional abuse that I have done both in the immediate situation, which brought me here, and in the entire relationship (Not taking the other person's feelings into account, being inconsiderate, ignoring them, depreciating them as a person, belittling their contribution or value, making fun of them, not listening. Stalking, violating court orders, unwanted contact, humiliation, degradation, causing embarrassment, depression, suicide, mental illness, poor self-esteem.)?

_____

Why was that wrong? _____

_____

What were the irrational thoughts I used to justify what I did? _____

_____

What are my shortcomings or inadequacies which motivated me to do something abusive?_____

_____

What do I need to do to fix those shortcomings or inadequacies so that I don't do this again? _____

_____

What would non-controlling, non-abusive, and non-violent alternative beliefs be? _____

_____

What was the damage or effect it had on the other person? _____

_____

What could I have done that wouldn't have been emotionally abusive? _____

_____

What should my apology be? _____

_____

What should my amends be?_____

_____

What are the apology and amends I have done this week for this abuse? _____

_____

What are the non-abusive, non-controlling alternatives to emotional abuse (Praise, encouragement, emotional support, valuing them, acknowledging them) which I have practiced this week?

_____

_____

Name_____ Submitted ___/___/___

ASSIGNMENT ELEVEN
VERBAL ABUSE

What are the forms of verbal abuse that I have done both in the immediate situation, which brought me here, and in the entire relationship (Bad language, name calling, labels, ridicule, rudeness, and sarcasm. Yelling Screaming, assaulting their value as a person to the point of causing emotional or psychological damage)?

_____

Why was that wrong? _____

_____

What were the irrational thoughts I used to justify what I did? _____

_____

What would non-controlling, non-abusive, and non-violent alternative beliefs be? _____

_____

What are my shortcomings or inadequacies which motivated me to do something abusive?

_____

_____

What do I need to do to fix those shortcomings or inadequacies so that I don't do this again?

_____

_____

What was the damage or effect it had on the other person? _____

_____

What could I have done that wouldn't have been verbally abusive? _____

_____

What should my apology be? _____

_____

What should my amends be?_____

_____

What are the apology and amends I have done this week for this abuse? _____
_____

What are the non-abusive, non-controlling alternatives to verbal abuse (Using words to calm and sooth, creating an atmosphere of respect and safety, of being valued and heard) which I have used this week?

_____

Name_____ Submitted ___/___/___

ASSIGNMENT TWELVE
PSYCHOLOGICAL ABUSE

What are the forms of psychological abuse that I have done both in the immediate situation, which brought me here, and in the entire relationship (Inconsistency, incompleteness, being hard to read, not telling the "whole story", not taking "no" for an answer, Leaving the other person in a "one down" position because they can't read you, don't know where you stand, can't predict what you will do next. "Crazy making", changing your story. Violating NCO. Bait and switch strategies, lying, manipulation, inconsistencies, "crazy making" to the point of making the other person doubt their sanity, stalking, property damage)?

_____

_____

Why was that wrong? _____

_____

What were the irrational thoughts I used to justify what I did? _____

_____

What would non-controlling, non-abusive, and non-violent alternative beliefs be? _____

_____

What are my shortcomings or inadequacies which motivated me to do something abusive?

_____

_____

What do I need to do to fix those shortcomings or inadequacies so that I don't do this again?

_____

_____

What was the damage or effect it had on the other person? _____

_____

What could I have done that wouldn't have been psychologically abusive? _____

_____

What should my apology be? _____

_____

What should my amends be?_____

_____

What are the apology and amends I have done this week for this abuse? _____
_____

What are the opposites of psychological abuse, which are non-abusive, non-controlling, which I have practiced this week? (Being consistent, predictable and reliable, telling the whole truth. Not using any manipulation or trickery even when you could get away with it.)_____

_____

_____

Name_____ Submitted ___/___/___

ASSIGNMENT THIRTEEN
MINIMIZATION, DENIAL AND BLAME

What are the forms of minimization, denial and blame that I have done both in the immediate situation, which brought me here, and in the entire relationship (Brushing off the effect you have on the other person, not acknowledging the wrongness of what you have done, or the damage you have done. Openly denying that you did something, lying and deceiving, minimizing the effect it had, blaming it on the other person or something else. Boldly blaming what you did or it's effects on the other person, denying that it happened, denying responsibility for what you did)?

_____

Why was that wrong? _____

_____

What were the irrational thoughts I used to justify what I did? _____

_____

What would non-controlling, non-abusive, and non-violent alternative beliefs be? _____

_____

What are my shortcomings or inadequacies which motivated me to do something abusive?

_____

_____

What do I need to do to fix those shortcomings or inadequacies so that I don't do this again?

_____

_____

What was the damage or effect it had on the other person? _____

_____

What could I have done which wouldn't be minimizing, denying, or blameful? _____

_____

What should my apology be? _____

_____

What should my amends be? Specifically, how am I going to correct all the things I minimized or denied? In what ways am I going to tell people the truth to correct the record?

_____

_____

What are the apology and amends I have done this week for my minimization, denial and blame?

_____

_____

What are the non-abusive, non-controlling opposites of minimization, denial and blame (Honesty and openness about what you did, honestly admitting to the damage it caused and making sincere amends to repair the damage when possible. Absence of blame.) which I have practiced this week? _____

_____

Name_____ Submitted ___/___/___

ASSIGNMENT FOURTEEN
USE OF FEAR, INTIMIDATION, COERCION AND THREATS

What are the forms of fear, intimidation, coercion and threats (Doing things that frighten or intimidate, subtle implication of threat, use of coercion such as "if you do this you'll get that". Openly using threats and fear to get your way or control the other person. Making them feel unsafe and having to "walk on eggshells". Threats to friends, pets, property. Threats that are carried out, no longer any negotiations on a level playing field, the other person no longer has a reasonable, free voice in what they say and do. Property damage, abuse of pets, threats to friends or family.) that I have done both in the immediate situation, which brought me here, and in the entire relationship?

_____

Why was that wrong? _____

_____

What were the irrational thoughts I used to justify what I did? _____

_____

What would non-controlling, non-abusive, and non-violent alternative beliefs be? _____

_____

What are my shortcomings or inadequacies which motivated me to do something abusive?

_____

_____

What do I need to do to fix those shortcomings or inadequacies so that I don't do this again?

_____

_____

What was the damage or effect it had on the other person? _____

_____

What could I have done that wouldn't have been intimidating, coercive, or frightening?

_____

_____

What should my apology be? _____

_____

What should my amends be? How can I repair the fear I caused?

_____

_____

What are the apology and amends I have done this week for this abuse? _____

_____

What are the non-abusive, non-controlling opposites of intimidation and fear (Create an environment of trust and safety in which choices are made freely and there is no issue of coercion.) which I have practiced this week? ____

_____

_____

Name_____ Submitted ___/___/___

ASSIGNMENT FIFTEEN
SOCIAL ABUSE AND ISOLATION

What are the forms of social abuse and isolation (Censoring or passing judgment on what the other person can do, where they can go, who they should or can see, talk to, associate with, etc. Pulling away from them emotionally, not being emotionally available. Open efforts to control or monitor their activities, phone calls, what they read, who they associate with. Interfering with friendships, activities or associations. Stalking. The other person is a virtual prisoner. One or more friends, family or activities has been deemed unacceptable or unavailable. Threats to friends or family.) that I have done both in the immediate situation, which brought here, and in the entire relationship?

_____

Why was that wrong? _____

_____

What were the irrational thoughts I used to justify what I did? _____

_____

What would non-controlling, non-abusive, and non-violent alternative beliefs be?

_____

_____

What are my shortcomings or inadequacies which motivated me to do something abusive?

_____

_____

What do I need to do to fix those shortcomings or inadequacies so that I don't do this again?

_____

_____

What was the damage or effect it had on the other person? _____

_____

What could I have done that wouldn't have been socially abusive or isolating?

_____

_____

What should my apology be? _____
_____

What should my amends be? How can I repair the relationships which I damaged? _____
_____

What are the apology and amends I have done this week for this abuse? _____
_____

What are the non-abusive, non-controlling opposites of social abuse and isolation (Open support and encouragement of all of their friendships, family relationships and activities. They feel safe, valued and supported) which I have practiced this week?_____
_____
_____

Name_____ Submitted ___/___/___

ASSIGNMENT SIXTEEN
USING CHILDREN

In what ways have I used, neglected, or manipulated children (Playing the children off against the other parent, making negative comments about the other parent. Using harsh physical, verbal or emotional punishments with the children. Use of physical punishment, talking badly about the other parent, lobbying the children to take your side against the other parent, not sharing in parenting responsibilities, reducing the children to being bargaining chips, expecting the children to take sides, manipulating visitations, using visitations to verbally abuse the other parent.) both in the immediate situation, which brought me here, and in the entire relationship? In what ways have I directly or indirectly let their needs be second place?

_____

Why was that wrong? _____

_____

What were the irrational thoughts I used to justify what I did? _____

_____

What are my shortcomings or inadequacies which motivated me to do something abusive?_____

_____

What do I need to do to fix those shortcomings or inadequacies so that I don't do this again? _____

_____

What would non-controlling, non-abusive, and non-violent alternative beliefs be?

_____

_____

What was the damage or effect it had on the children?_____

_____

What could I have done which would have kept the children from being involved or affected? Which would have shown more responsible parenting?

_____

_____

What should my apology be? _____

_____

What should my amends be? _____
_____

What are the apology and amends I have done this week for this abuse? _____
_____

What are the non-abusive, non-controlling opposites of using the children (Sharing parenting in an open, responsible way, supporting the other parent. Using rewards, not punishments with the children) which I have practiced this week? _____
_____
_____

Name_____ Submitted ___/___/___

ASSIGNMENT SEVENTEEN
FINANCIAL ABUSE

What are the forms of financial abuse that I have done both in the immediate situation, which brought me here, and in the entire relationship? _____

_____

_____

Why was that wrong? _____

_____

What were the irrational thoughts I used to justify what I did? _____

_____

What would non-controlling, non-abusive, and non-violent alternative beliefs be? _____

_____

What are my shortcomings or inadequacies which motivated me to do something abusive? _____

_____

What do I need to do to fix those shortcomings or inadequacies so that I don't do this again? _____

_____

What was the damage or effect it had on the other person? _____

_____

What could I have done that wouldn't have been financially abusive? What would have been more financially responsible? _____

_____

What should my apology be? _____

_____

What should my amends be?_____

_____

What are the apology and amends I have done this week for this abuse? _____
_____

                                                                               Name_____ Submitted ___/___/___

LESSON EIGHTEEN:

SOCIAL INSTITUTIONS WHICH SUPPORT CONTROL, ABUSE, AND VIOLENCE

There are some ethnic groups in India, and in Indian communities outside of India, where it is not uncommon for men who are disappointed in their wives, or the dowries they are paid for marrying their wives, to cover them with kerosene and burn them to death. Thousands of women per year are killed that way.

This is extremely rare in the United States and the primary cultures which operate here. Most people here would be horrified at this practice, yet many socially acceptable young men in that culture do this.

In some parts of Africa it is acceptable to "circumcise" young woman by cutting off parts of their genitals. That is extremely rare and illegal in the United States. We would find it horrifying. Yet many socially acceptable men in those cultures are involved in this practice.

But by the same token there are many parts of our everyday life which socially acceptable men indulge in which people from those other cultures would find equally horrifying. The sexual practices, language, dress and social lives which are common in our culture would be completely forbidden, even unthinkable, in many cultures. Many of the things we do everyday would be considered inexcusably violent or abusive.

Control, abuse, and violence rarely occur except when the culture or subculture of the individual accept, endorse, excuse, justify or tolerate the abuse or violence.

Our culture and society support abuse and violence in many ways

- Many of our religious groups strongly oppose child abuse laws on the grounds that they believe that the Christian Bible condones and even recommends physical abuse of children.
- Many religious persuasions, to one degree or another, condone or encourage patriarchal family structures which place men in a position of power over women and children.
- Our schools overlook serious crimes of violence and sexual crimes by their male athletes against both male and female students. Hazing is quite legal in most schools and states.
- For many years our schools openly practiced physical abuse of children.
- Our media strongly praise and idolize violent, abusive heroes.
- Special laws had to be passed to get our police departments and courts to enforce laws about assault in family cases.
    - Until the mid 20th century it was not illegal to abuse your child up to and including the point of permanent injury
    - It was not illegal to rape your wife until 1979

- In the world of business, using unfair business practices to destroy other people or companies is heavily rewarded. CEOs get huge bonuses for laying off thousands of innocent workers. Whoever wins, no matter what the degree of abuse they employ, gets financially rewarded.
    o If I broke into your house and stole $1,000 from you, I would go to prison for many years, but if I run a company which wipes out $100,000 of your retirement account just so I can give myself a bonus, that's okay.
    o If a poor young man in the ghetto steals a twelve year old Toyota with a bad transmission, he would go to prison for up to nine years. If a businessman manipulates stocks and costs thousand of people billions of dollars he gets to go to a country club for six months. And, sometimes, he gets to keep the money.
- The therapy professions have for a long time blamed family abuse on family or marital problems, thus blaming the victim for the offender abusing them, blaming the children for getting hit. Also, it has been a common practice for many years to excuse an offender's behavior as being the result of a bad childhood, mental or emotional problems, etc. and thus getting them off of legal charges, or at least not being held responsible for changing their behavior.
- It is now a common practice in domestic violence cases to have the victim get a psychological evaluation in order to dismiss the charges against the perpetrator.

As mentioned earlier there are quite a few ideas and beliefs which are endorsed by our overall culture which support and condone control, abuse and violence.

- Beliefs in the roles of men versus women
- Beliefs in provocation
- Beliefs in the excusability of what we do when drunk, angry, tired, etc.

It is amazing how often people will come into the program, terribly upset and telling me:

- "I shouldn't have to be here, my buddy said it was her fault" (victim blaming)
- "My minister said it doesn't matter what I did, she doesn't have the right to break up the family" (men can possess women)
- "I shouldn't have to be here, I haven't done anything half my neighbors haven't done" (modeling of violence)
- "How can she say I'm abusive? I haven't hit her in years. The worst I've done is threatened to hit her." (verbal abuse and threats are okay)
- "This is bull. She called the police on me three times before and I wasn't arrested, so what I did isn't illegal." (enabling by the legal system)
- "I shouldn't be here. I got an evaluation that said I was drunk at the time and all I should have is alcohol treatment." Or "I shouldn't be here, I got an evaluation by a psychiatrist that said I was depressed so all I need is antidepressants." (both are enabling by the treatment community)

What are the institutions, beliefs and supports that you used to rationalize, justify or excuse your anger, control, abuse or violence?

ASSIGNMENT EIGHTEEN
SOCIAL SUPPORTS FOR CONTROL, ABUSE AND/OR VIOLENCE

WAC 388-60-0245 (7)

These are the forms of control, abuse, or violence which I saw modeled in my home or community; _____
_____

My culture, or family, or subgroup, sports, or religion modeled these forms of power, abuse or control_____
_____

These are the forms of abuse, control or violence I saw modeled in the media;
_____
_____

These were the attitudes about men's abuse of women which I heard or saw in church, school, athletic personalities, the media, etc. _____
_____

These were the things I saw other men or boys getting away with, which were controlling, abusive, or violent toward women, including financial and legal abuse _____
_____

Because of all those things, this is what I learned about control, abuse or violence toward family members or loved ones; _____
_____

These are the responses I got from my friends, family, support group, church, the legal system, my lawyer, the police, the courts, other counselors etc. *which condoned, excused, enabled, rationalized or justified my control, abuse or violence*_____
_____

The ways in which I took advantage of those negative supports, or those chances to enable, condone, excuse or justify what I did were;_____
_____

These are the responses I got which took a clear position that *control, abuse, and violence are never acceptable;* ___
_____

These are the negative consequences I have experienced at home, in my extended family, from friends, social institutions, churches, school, at work, and in the legal system, for having been controlling, abusive, or violent_____

_____

Here is what I can do to reeducate the people in my family, extended family, community, church, school, workplace, or in the legal system, that control, abuse and violence are never justified _____

_____

And here is what I have already done to reeducate those people or institutions?

_____

_____

Name_____ Submitted ___/___/___

ASSIGNMENT NINETEEN
ABUSE USING THE LEGAL SYSTEM

Racism was once legal in this country, but that didn't make it okay to own slaves. You were still a slave owner. You were still inherently abusive. But it was perfectly legal.

Hitler used his criminal and civil courts to justify killing many Jews on the basis of crimes that they were alleged to have committed. That didn't make it right. But it was legal.

Up until 1979 it was legal to rape your wife. If you forced your wife to have sex, it wasn't a crime. But the effects on your victim were the same. Legal or not, it was abuse.

Until 1979 most domestic violence wasn't against the law. So, before that, it was legal, but it was still abuse. It sure says something about the legal system that they had to pass a law that said laws against assault had to be enforced in family situations.

It wasn't mandatory that the law be enforced until 1985. It sure says something about the legal system that they actually had to pass a law that said you have to enforce the law that says you have to enforce the law against assault when it was in a family situation.

According to British Common Law, which is the basis for our common law which became the basis for our laws, not only was it legal to beat your child, but, if you were beating your child and you asked a passer by to hold your child while you beat him and they refused, that passer by was guilty of the crime of not assisting. But that didn't make the beating any less abusive nor did it lessen the effects on the child.

In other words, just because something is legal doesn't necessarily mean it isn't abusive. In fact, the legal system has long been one of the main tools that abusers have used to establish and use power over their victims;

- Whites over minorities
- Men over women
- Rich over poor
- Lawyers over everyone

Consequently, the legal system can be used to force our will on other people in a way which violates their basic rights, just like any other method for abusing someone. We can use it to lie about our partners or ex-partners. We can use it to deprive them of financial resources they have coming to them. We can use it to take away their children unjustly. We can even just plain use the legal system to outspend them. We can use it to harass them, slander them, cost them their careers, turn their friends against them.

Thus, a part of this program is to educate you as to what abuse using the legal system is, and to require you to spend twelve continuous months without using that form of abuse, just like you have to spend twelve continuous months without any other form of abuse.

It's very difficult to explain or define abuse through the legal system, so here are some examples;

- Taking legal actions against the victim in retribution for them holding you accountable for your actions
- Making false charges, for any reason
- Outspending the victim until they can't afford to defend themselves.
- Lying in any legal document
- In any legal document or action attempting to blame or slander the victim

- Attempting to use the legal system to coerce or force this program or any friend, ally or caregiver for the victim into changing their story or colluding with you against the victim
- Not following the letter and spirit of any court orders.
- Filing unnecessary motions or attempting to either stall or overwhelm the victim with legal actions
- Stalling
- Withholding information
- Attempting to get a No Contact Order, Protection Order, or Restraining Order dropped when the victim doesn't want you to.
- Attempting to get information from the victim or from others who don't want to give you that information.
- Attempting to get a gag order on the treatment program
- Denying in court that you did what you did or contradicting in court or court documents what you have said in your responsibility statements here, or coming close to
- Lying in court for any reason
- Saying one thing in criminal court and another thing in family court
- Agreeing that you did the crime in order to get certain consideration from the court then coming into group and saying you didn't do it, such as taking an Alford plea then coming here and saying that you didn't do what you pled to.
- Using the legal system to get special breaks for abusive behavior.
- Harassing the victim through your attorney, such as having your attorney contact the victim to deliver thinly veiled threatening messages.

These are just some of the ways people commonly use the legal system to abuse or control victims of domestic violence without ever touching them. It is no less abusive. You would certainly feel abused if it happened to you.

When you are in a domestic violence program, you are expected to show that you can run your life and your affairs in a responsible, non-blaming, non-abusive way. This isn't different than being in an alcohol program. We have a right to drink, but if you are attempting to show that you can remain sober, you have to abstain from drinking, even in situations where it's okay for other people to drink. If you are in a domestic violence program, you need to abstain from the use of control, abuse, or violence, including all forms of fear or force, even if it happens to be legal. Legal isn't necessarily the same as non abusive or controlling.

Doing any of the above activities, or something which, in the eyes of the victim appear abusive or controlling, is abuse. You are here to show that you can abstain from control, abuse, violence and the use of fear or force.

Including forms of fear or force which are perfectly legal.

ASSIGNMENT NINETEEN
ABUSE THROUGH THE LEGAL SYSTEM

Have I ever used the legal system, criminal or civil, to force my will on the victim in this case (any of the behaviors noted above or similar behaviors)? _____

_____

Have I ever lied in a legal document, either on my own or with the collusion of an attorney or misrepresented the truth?_____

_____

Have I ever used the legal system to punish the victim or anyone else in this case for the steps they have taken? ___

_____

Have I ever deliberately gone slow on my legal obligations to another person?

_____

_____

Have I ever caused harm to the other person through my use of the legal system?

_____

_____

What are my shortcomings or inadequacies which motivated me to do something abusive?_____

_____

What do I need to do to fix those shortcomings or inadequacies so that I don't do this again? _____

_____

What is the damage I have done, directly or indirectly, to the victim in this case?

_____

_____

What are the amends I need to take to repair the damage, replace what I have taken, or to correct any lies or misrepresentations I have done in this case?

_____

_____

What are the amends I have done this week to repair the damage I have done through the legal system? _____

_____

Name_____ Submitted ___/___/___

CHAPTER FOUR

LEGAL ASPECTS OF FAMILY VIOLENCE

LESSON TWENTY:

LEGAL AND OTHER CONSEQUENCES OF DOMESTIC VIOLENCE

WAC 388-60-0245 (8)

There are numerous laws, both criminal and civil, which make domestic violence illegal and which provide legal consequences for committing various acts of domestic violence.

It is important to note that most forms of domestic violence are legal, in that they aren't specifically against the law. Consequently, just because something isn't against the law doesn't mean it's okay. Spousal rape was legal until 1979, but that doesn't mean it was okay until then. Just legal.

RCW 26.50.150 (1) (a) defines domestic violence as
"… Physical harm, bodily injury, assault or the infliction of fear of imminent physical harm, bodily injury or assault between family or household members; or (b) sexual assault of one family or household member by another."

RCW 10.99.020 (5) defines domestic violence as
"includes but is not limited to any of the following crimes when committed by one family or household member against another"
    (a) Assault in the first degree
    (b) Assault in the second degree
    (c) Assault in the third degree
    (d) Assault in the fourth degree;
    (e) Drive-by shooting
    (f) Reckless endangerment
    (g) Coercion
    (h) Burglary in the first degree
    (i) Burglary in the second degree
    (j) Criminal trespass in the first degree
    (k) Criminal trespass in the second degree
    (l) Malicious mischief in the first degree
    (m) Malicious mischief in the second degree
    (n) Malicious mischief in the third degree
    (o) Kidnapping in the first degree
    (p) Kidnapping in the second degree
    (q) Unlawful imprisonment

(r) Violation of the provisions of a restraining order, no-contact order, or protection order restraining or enjoining the person or restraining the person from going onto the grounds of or entering a residence, workplace, school, or day care, or prohibiting the person from knowingly coming within, or knowingly remaining within, a specified distance of a location
(s) Rape in the first degree
(t) Rape in the second degree
(u) Residential burglary
(v) Stalking
(w) Interference with the reporting of domestic violence

Consequently, just because you don't simply hit someone in the nose with a closed fist doesn't mean it isn't domestic violence.

What does it take to get arrested? There is a legal term which relies on common sense called "probable cause", which means that an officer has reason to believe that a crime has occurred. The legal definition of probable cause is in RCW 10.99.030 (3) (a) which states "when a peace officer responds to a domestic violence call and has probable cause to believe that a crime has been committed the peace officer shall exercise arrest powers …"

Next, RCW 10.99.020 (3) defines who a "family or household member" is. It's not just someone you are currently married to.

(3) "Family or household members" means spouses, former spouses, persons who have a child in common regardless of whether they have been married or have lived together at any time, adult persons related by blood or marriage, adult persons who are presently residing together or who have resided together in the past, persons sixteen years of age or older who are presently residing together or who have resided together in the past and who have or have had a dating relationship, persons sixteen years of age or older with whom a person sixteen years of age or older has or has had a dating relationship, and persons who have a biological or legal parent-child relationship, including stepparents and stepchildren and grandparents and grandchildren.
(4) "Dating relationship" has the same meaning as in RCW 26.50.010.
(8) "Victim" means a family or household member who has been subjected to domestic violence.

It is also important to remember what you are pleading to in court.

Any number of poorly informed attorneys fail to make it clear to you what is going on in court. Most importantly, they can create the impression that you can cut a deal in court and get away without admitting guilt or paying the penalties for being guilty.

RCW 10.99.080 (4) For the purposes of this section, "convicted" includes a plea of guilty, a finding of guilt regardless of whether the imposition of the sentence is deferred or any part of the penalty is suspended, or the levying of a fine. For the purposes of this section, "domestic violence" has the same meaning as that term is defined under RCW and includes violations of equivalent local ordinances.

This means that pleading guilty is pleading guilty, whether it is an Alford plea, or pleading guilty to a lesser charge. You are still pleading guilty and can't get out of it. It also means that any sort of deferred prosecution, which includes a Stipulated Order of Continuance, is still a plea of guilty. If you want to take advantage of one of these legal options, you still have to take the responsibility which comes with it. There is no free lunch.

Finally, recent changes in the law allow the court to fine you up to an additional $100 to go into a fund to help victims of domestic violence;

RCW 10.99.080 (1) All superior courts, and courts organized under Title 3 may impose a penalty assessment not to exceed one hundred dollars on any person convicted of a crime involving domestic violence. The assessment shall be in addition to, and shall not supersede, any other penalty, restitution, fines, or costs provided by law.

What does this mean in terms of our everyday lives?

What this means, is that the police departments and courts are very clear about enforcing the laws about domestic violence;

- Doing virtually any act of violence, to anyone you have been in a domestic relationship with, not just hitting, is a crime.
    - Interfering with the other person's efforts to call 911, in any way, shape, or form, becomes a separate crime in and of itself.
- That crime is punishable by *at the very least* up to one year in prison and *at the very least* up to a $5,000 fine.
- A third misdemeanor becomes a class "C" felony and conviction can mean prison time, loss of the right to bear arms, loss of the right to vote, and being on the state list as a felon for life.
- Violation of a no-contact order, a restraining order, or a civil order of protection, for any reason, is a crime;
    - It doesn't matter if the other person violates the court order first; if you do it, it's at the least a misdemeanor
        - According to the law
            - b) " ... You can be arrested even if any person protected by the order invites or allows you to violate the order's prohibitions. You have the sole responsibility to avoid or refrain from violating the order's provisions. Only the court can change the order."
    - If you commit an act of assault or malicious mischief while violating the court order, it becomes a class "C" felony.
- It is important to note that the preface to this section is that the written law "includes but is not limited to any of the following crimes when committed by one family or household member against another"
    - In other words, if you violate the rights of another person in a way which isn't specifically listed as a crime, it can still be a domestic violence crime if it is a violation in the spirit of the law.
- You can't get out of the legal consequences with some fancy footwork on the part of the attorneys involved; unless you are innocent, plead innocent, and are found innocent by the judge or the jury, you will have to face the legal and personal consequences of the acts you have done or pled to.

ASSIGNMENT TWENTY
LEGAL CONSEQUENCES OF DOMESTIC VIOLENCE

Are there forms or instances of domestic violence which are illegal but for which I didn't get arrested but could have? _____

Assault _____

Drive by shooting _____

Reckless endangerment _____

Coercion _____

Burglary _____

Criminal trespass _____

Malicious mischief _____

Kidnapping _____

Unlawful imprisonment _____

Violation of the provisions of a restraining order, no-contact order, or protection order location
_____

Rape _____

Stalking _____

Residential burglary _____

Interference with the reporting of domestic violence _____

What is the sum of all of the maximum penalties I could have experienced if all of those events or instances had been reported and if I'd been arrested and charged? _____

Name_____ Submitted ___/___/___

LESSON TWENTY ONE:

COURT ORDERS PERTAINING TO DOMESTIC VIOLENCE

There are four types of court orders which can be issued to prevent further acts of violence.

TYPE OF ORDER	FORMS OF RELIEF	EFFECTS ON THE VIOLATOR
No Contact Order, also known as an NCO (RCW 10.99.020)	No contact with the victim. This includes no third party contacts. This is done by the judge and does not "belong" to the victim. In a sense it is an alternative to jail in order to keep the parties completely separate.	Mandatory arrest. Up to $5,000 fine and up to 1 year in jail.
Civil Order of Protection (RCW 26.50)	No contact with the victim. Exclusion from residence. Custody of children. Other provisions. This order is done at the request of the victim, and is a civil order, but violating it is a criminal offense	Mandatory arrest, civil contempt.
Civil Restraining Order (RCW 26.09.060)	No contact with the victim. Other provisions at the discretion of the victim.	Mandatory arrest Civil contempt Up to $5,000 fine and up to 1 year in jail.
Civil Anti-Harassment Order (RCW 10.14)	No contact with the victim	Mandatory Arrest Up to $5,000 fine and up to 1 year in jail.

- A court order is valid even if the victim "gives permission" for you to violate it.
- Violation can include any form of contact, through a third party, even sending a Christmas card; no means no means no.
- Committing an act of assault or malicious mischief in violation of any of these orders is an automatic felony.
- A third violation of a court order becomes a class "C" felony

ASSIGNMENT TWENTY ONE
COURT ORDERS PERTAINING TO DOMESTIC VIOLENCE

What are the four kinds of court orders that relate to domestic violence cases?

1. _____

2. _____

3. _____

4. _____

Which ones come from a criminal offense or are part of a criminal action? _____
_____

Which ones are civil? _____
_____

When can a victim give permission to violate or make an exception to a court order? _____
_____

What are some forms of third party contacts which are permissible? _____
_____

When have I violated a court order in any way? _____
_____

What could the penalties have been for those violations? _____
_____

Name_____ Submitted ___/___/___

SECTION FOUR

THE INVENTORIES

LESSON TWENTY TWO:

WHAT ARE ALL THE FORMS OF ABUSE YOU HAVE USED AND WHAT ARE THE ALTERNATIVES YOU ARE COMMITTING TO USING IN THE FUTURE

WAC 388-60-0245 (8)

At this point in your program you have spent several months going over all the forms of violence you have used. Go through all the assignments and list all the forms of control, abuse or violence you have used, and the non-controlling, non-abusive, non-violent alternatives you are committing to using in the future. Here are some examples, which can help you in this part of the inventory;

Form of abuse, control, or violence   Alternatives

Form of abuse, control, or violence	Alternatives
PHYSICAL ASSAULT	Physical respect and comfort
SEXUAL ABUSE,	Sexual respect and intimacy, creating an atmosphere of comfort and dignity and sexual fulfillment.
GENDER ABUSE	Genuine equality of the sexes, respecting the rights, needs and feelings of all genders and gender orientations in an atmosphere of trust and safety.
EMOTIONAL ABUSE	Praise, encouragement, genuine emotional support, valuing the other person and acknowledging them.
VERBAL ABUSE	Using words to calm and sooth, creating an atmosphere of respect and safety, of being valued and heard.
PSYCHOLOGICAL ABUSE	Being consistent, predictable and reliable, telling the truth and the whole truth. Not using any manipulation or trickery even when you could get away with it.
MINIMIZATION, DENIAL AND BLAME	Honesty and openness about what you did, honestly admitting to the damage it caused and making sincere amends to repair the damage when possible. Absence of blame.
USE OF FEAR, INTIMIDATION, COERCION AND THREATS	Create an environment of trust and safety in which choices are made freely and there is no issue of coercion.
SOCIAL ABUSE, ISOLATION	Open support and encouragement of all of their friendships, family relationships and activities. They feel safe, valued and supported.

FINANCIAL ABUSE WAC 388-60-0235 (10)	Sharing in all financial decisions in an equal way, sharing decision-making and information and living up to reasonable financial and material expectations.
USING CHILDREN	Sharing parenting in an open, responsible way, supporting the other parent. Not involving children in issues between the parents.

So that this commitment is meaningful we ask that you have someone in your life not connected to this program witness your commitment by cosigning your commitment.

ASSIGNMENT TWENTY TWO
WHAT ARE ALL THE FORMS OF ABUSE I HAVE USED AND THE ALTERNATIVES I AM COMMITTING TO USING IN THE FUTURE

All of the forms and examples of control, abuse, or violence which I have listed in all of the other exercises, including any that weren't included in the other exercises	The healthy alternatives to that control, abuse, or violence I am committing to using in the future.

I _____ am hereby committing to not using any forms of control, abuse or violence in my life or in my relationships. I am committing to these inventories and these forms of non-controlling, non-abusive, non-violent forms of behavior.

_____ ___/___/___ _____ ___/___/___
(My name) (Witnessed by)

LESSON TWENTY THREE:
DEALING WITH OUR INADEQUACIES

As we have discussed throughout the book, and in the group therapy program, using fear, force, coercion, control, abuse or violence is an admission that we are inadequate. Each time we use some form of abuse we are admitting that we aren't smart enough, strong enough, brave enough or skilled enough to do something that would make more sense. For each act of abuse we have committed in our lifetimes, there is a weakness or shortcoming which motivated us to use abuse.

And that's what we are here to fix.

All of the exercises in the DOMESTIC VIOLENCE section of this book included a question about what your inadequacy or shortcoming was which motivated that act. For example, you may have yelled at the other person (verbal abuse) because you didn't have the verbal skills to express your feelings in an adult way. A lack of verbal skill would be the inadequacy.

It's good to know what our weaknesses are so that we can work on them. It isn't enough to say "I'm not a good money manager". We have to take the next step and commit to learning more about money management by going to one of the consumer counseling agencies, or taking a class, or hiring an accountant, or even just asking a friend to help.

For this exercise, go through all the exercises in the DOMESTIC VIOLENCE section of the book and list all the inadequacies or shortcomings which have accounted for any and all forms of control, abuse or violence you have used in the left column.

In the right column, list the action plan you will use for fixing those inadequacies or shortcomings. For example, if you listed "I am impatient and self centered" list the things you will need to do in the next few years to become a patient, unselfish person. For example, you could say "I will practice patience when listening to my family. I will practice giving without thinking of what I will get back. When I am selfish or impatient I will immediately catch myself, stop, apologize, and make amends."

This can be difficult because some of the shortcomings could take many years and many steps to overcoming. But be as detailed as possible.

As with ASSIGNMENT TWENTY TWO; THE FORMS OF ABUSE I HAVE USED AND THE ALTERNATIVES I AM COMMITTING TO USING, we ask that you have a witness cosign your commitment to this long-range plan. Because we want you to get as much support as possible for your change we ask that it be a different person than the one who witnessed your commitment to the behavioral changes in Assignment Twenty Two.

ASSIGNMENT TWENTY THREE
DEALING WITH OUR INADEQUACIES

The inadequacies or shortcomings I have identified in Assignments 6-19 which account for my decisions to use control, abuse or violence	The long-range plans I need to follow to fix those inadequacies or shortcomings

I _____ am hereby committing to following the above action plan to address my own personal problems so that I don't use control, abuse, or violence against another person.

_____ ___/___/___   _____ ___/___/___
(My name)   (Witnessed by)

LESSON TWENTY FOUR:

BEING A SAFE PERSON

To truly change our patterns of abusive, controlling behavior we have to be the kind of person who is safe to be with. The absence of bad behavior isn't enough. We can't just be content saying "I haven't hit you in two years, so shut up and stop being afraid."

We have to live differently. We have to live like the sort of person that it's safe for our loved ones to be with. To confide in. To trust.

There is quite a history of people deliberately cultivating the traits they need to face the tasks they have to face.

- In the Twelve Step Traditions they have the Serenity Prayer; God grant me the strength to change the things I can change, the serenity to accept the things I cannot change and the wisdom to know the difference."
- The Boy Scouts have their Scout Law. A Scout is trustworthy, loyal, helpful, friendly, courteous, kind, obedient, cheerful, thrifty, brave, clean and reverent.
- The Christian Bible has the Beatitudes; Blessed are the poor, the meek, they who mourn, they that hunger and thirst after justice, the merciful, the clean of heart, the peacemakers, and they that suffer persecution for justices' sake.
- The Buddhists have The Eightfold Path; Right View, Right Intention, Right Speech, Right Action, Right Livelihood, Right Effort, Right Mindfulness, and Right Concentration.
- Two psychologists, Cloud and Townsend, in an effort to help people find partners with whom they would be safe, came up with a list of the traits of safe people and the traits of unsafe people. Even though it was intended for past victims of bad relationships to pick safer partners, we can use it so that we can learn the traits we need to cultivate in order to be the kind of person who can be a safe person for our current partner to be with or, if that relationship is over, for our next partner to be with.
- William J. Bennett published "The Book of Virtues" to illustrate a plethora of virtues we should all learn and practice.

The chart, below, is one such list of traits. I would encourage all of us to spend a fair amount of our lives learning what the traits are that we need to develop, and come up with our own list. However, in the short run, for your current assignment, please review the Safe People list and answer the questions on your assignment form.

As with the last two exercises, we are asking you to get a witness to your commitment to making these changes, and a different witness than the other two exercises.

INTERPERSONAL TRAITS OF UNSAFE PEOPLE VERSUS SAFE PEOPLE[2]

UNSAFE PEOPLE	SAFE PEOPLE
1. Avoid closeness instead of connecting.	1. Prioritize connecting and closeness.
2. Only concerned about "I" instead of "we", not responding in an empathic manner. If they help it is to get something later, make contact when they need something, and respond to the needs of other superficially and in a utilitarian manner.	2. Concerned about the connection with others, they are empathic and act on their empathy.
3. Resist freedom in others instead of encouraging it. Don't accept "no" for an answer. May withdraw emotionally when others set limits, attempting to make the other person feel guilty for setting limits, don't accept separate life and interests in the other person.	3. Accept and cultivate the freedom and autonomy of those around them, take "no" for an answer without being resistant or resentful.
4. Flatter us instead of confronting us, thus leaving us without the information we need to work and live with them safely and respectfully.	4. Tell us what we need to know even if it hurts, but don't do it in a hurtful or self serving manner.
5. Condemn us instead of forgiving us.	5. They know our failings and do not minimize or excuse them, but forgive us genuinely and let it go.
6. Stay in parent/child roles instead of relating as equals. We feel alternately like a child, like we are supposed to parent them, but seldom feel on an equal footing with them.	6. They relate as equals, with neither party assuming responsibility for the other.
7. Unstable over time instead of being consistent and predictable.	7. Predictable and consistent.
8. They are a negative influence on us, and we tend to bring out our negative traits around them or behave in ways we don't like about ourselves.	8. They are a good influence on us over time, with us becoming more loving, honest, forgiving and mutual over time.
9. Gossip instead of keeping secrets. Don't respect or honor trust and boundaries.	9. Respect boundaries, privacy and secrets.

---

[2] Inspired by but liberally adapted from "Safe People" by Dr. Henry Cloud and Dr. John Townsend, 1995.

PERSONAL TRAITS OF UNSAFE PEOPLE VERSUS SAFE PEOPLE[3]

UNSAFE PEOPLE	**SAFE PEOPLE**
1. Give the appearance of "having it all together" instead of admitting their weaknesses, giving other people the experience of feeling disconnected, "one down", and weaker than they really are. Sometimes the others feel dependent on the "strong one", angry at them because of the tediousness of the facade, or the need to compete to reverse the role.	1. Safe people admit their vulnerabilities and weaknesses freely, allowing others to feel close to them without feeling disconnected, "one down", or weaker than they really are. Their relationships don't engender weakness, dependence or resentment nor is there competition to reverse the roles.
2. Defensive instead of being open to feedback.	2. Open to feedback without fear or defensiveness.
3. Self righteous instead of humble. See themselves as different from the rest of us fallible humans.	3. See their commonality with the rest of us without arrogance, or self-righteousness.
4. Apologize but don't change their behavior.	4. Apologies are accompanied with immediate and permanent changes in behavior. Motivated by respect, not just fear of "getting caught".
5. Avoid working on their problems instead of dealing with them. They don't admit that they have problems, do not admit when they have wronged someone, do not forgive people who have hurt them, avoid facing relationship problems directly and openly, do not treat others with empathy, are not open to confrontation from others, do not take responsibility for their own lives, blame other people for their problems, and do not want to share their problems with others to help them grow.	5. Are involved in the ongoing process of admitting to and dealing with problems, admit they have them without blaming others or circumstances and openly and actively seek input and support from others in the process of working on those problems, personally, interpersonally and in relationships. Treat others with empathy, are open to feedback and confrontation, and accept responsibility for their own lives.
6. Demand trust without earning it.	6. Earn trust without demanding it.
7. Believe they are perfect instead of admitting their faults and will go to considerable length to prove it.	7. Don't need to appear perfect.
8. Blame others instead of taking responsibility.	8. Accept responsibility for their own behavior and it's consequences without blaming other people or circumstances.
9. Lie instead of telling the truth and don't admit to their lies.	9. Tell the truth instead of lying and if they lie they admit it and rectify it immediately.

---

[3] Inspired by but liberally adapted from "Safe People" by Dr. Henry Cloud and Dr. John Townsend, 1995.

ASSIGNMENT TWENTY FOUR
BEING A SAFE PERSON

What are the traits of unsafe people which I have demonstrated, been, or used in the past, even if only in the eyes of my loved ones? _____

_____

_____

_____

_____

What are the traits of a safe person, which are the opposites of the unsafe traits, which I will commit to cultivating in myself in order to be a safer person to be around?

_____

_____

_____

_____

_____

What are the visible, demonstrable ways to which I will commit to show those changes in myself? _____

_____

_____

_____

_____

I _____ am hereby committing to making these changes to become a safe person to those in my life and in relationships with me.

_____

_____

_____

_____

_____ ___/___/___   _____ ___/___/___
         (My name)   (Witnessed by)

LESSON TWENTY FIVE:

THE RESPONSIBILITY LETTER

Now it's time to take all that you have learned and put it together in one place. And that place is the RESPONSIBILITY LETTER.

Whether or not you are still with the other person, the letter needs to be written as if you were going to give it to that person. This needs to be your masterpiece, the sum of everything you have learned in the program. You will present this letter to the group to pass the test of whether or not you are, and have been, taking responsibility for your actions. Be sure you bring enough copies for everyone so that they can go over it with you line by line. Be very sure you use the headings for each section, so we can review them with you one at a time. You will need to go through the letter as often as necessary for you to pass it completely. If you need more than one "re-write" you may be asked to give the group time in between attempts so that other participants can get group time.

If there are a number of people involved, even if they weren't part of your referral to the program, such as a wife and your children, you need to write a letter to each of them.

The measures for passing the RESPONSIBILITY LETTER are

- Are you able to describe and explain what happened and the context it happened in without
    - Minimization
    - Denial
    - Blame
    - Excuses
- Do you understand what it was that you did which was wrong and why it was wrong?
- Are you being honest about your motive for using anger, abuse, control, or violence instead of doing something that would have been more appropriate and non-violent?
- Do you understand all of the effects it had on the other person? And the effects of the whole context in which it occurred?
- Is your apology sincere and complete? Do you appear genuinely sorry for what you did and the effects it had on the other person?
- Are your amends appropriate and complete and are you doing them?

The letter is broken down into several sections so that we can be sure it is done thoroughly and accurately. Be sure to include the headings for the sections when you give it to the group, so we can address each section accurately.

1. What I did
2. The context within which it occurred
    a. How we met, the circumstances of our meeting
    b. How long the relationship lasted.
    c. The track record or history of anger, control, abuse, or violence I brought into the relationship, what I have done in the past or to or with other people.

    d. Other issues that I brought into the relationship, such as life struggles or personal difficulties or shortcomings.
    e. Forms of anger, control, abuse, and/or violence I have used in this relationship or toward other people during the relationship, in addition to what brought me here.
    f. Issues which have come about during this relationship, such as life changes, new problems, or stresses.
    g. Issues, experiences or circumstances which make you vulnerable to me so that the things that I do which abuse you are that much more hurtful or harmful to you.
    h. The history of all of these issues in the context of my whole life. Nothing happens in a vacuum. What does my control, abuse, or violence toward you have to do with the bigger picture of my life and my history?

3. My Motive for doing it. What I was thinking, what did I want to happen, what did I expect would happen, or the effect I expected this behavior would have on you.
4. Why that was wrong.
5. The effects it had on the you (for each and all of the victims);
    a. Physically
    b. Emotionally
    c. Financially
    d. Other ways
    6. My apology.
    7. My amends.

1. What I did

The first section needs to be an accurate and thorough description of what you did in the event that got you here. If you got here for a pattern of behavior, describe the whole pattern. Don't use this part of the letter to make a case for what a nice guy you are or for how the circumstances forced your hand. Just the facts. And don't make it about what the other person did. It's about what you did.

Right Way

"Dear Susan

The night after your birthday party I complained and found fault with you all the way home. When we got home I continued to pick on you. When you tried to go to bed to get away from my tirade I grabbed you and threw you on the couch and called you names. When you tried to get away a second time I hit you on the shoulder and knocked you down."

Wrong Way

"Dear Susan

I had been looking forward to your birthday party all year, and scrimped and saved and did without to get you a gift I knew that any wife would love. Even though your mother has treated me horribly as long as we've been married and has tried to break us up many times I went ahead with your wish to have the party at her house, with her friends and family, and not ours, because none of our friends like your mother. At the party you ignored me and I sat back politely and let you enjoy your party. When I tried to talk to you, you got huffy and went back to talking to the other people there. When your mother expected me to run errands, like taking out the garbage and taking dishes to the kitchen, I put up with the humiliation of being treated like hired help instead of the husband of the birthday girl.

When you opened the gifts you made a big deal out of everyone's gift but not the one that I got you. It was the nicest gift there. In fact, it was the nicest gift you've ever been given in your life. But you just pecked me on the cheek and went on like it was nothing.

I never said a word until on the way home you asked how I liked the party. All I said was that I pointed out my feelings were a little hurt and you went off like an animal. I suffered in silence. You yelled at me all the way home. I was patient. Once we got home you continued to yell insanely at me when all I did was defend myself for feeling slighted by your unjustified, selfish, materialistic attitude. I know I should not have pushed you onto the couch but I didn't know what else to do. The second time I pushed you was in self defense."

The reason this is the wrong way to do it is because this isn't about taking *her* inventory, it's about taking *yours*. This is a program about changing what *you* do. In this wrong way the writer is spending all of his time talking about what a nice guy he is and how the abuse was justified. It is full of minimization, denial and blame.

2. The context within which it occurred

Everything happens in a context. For example if I ask you to pick up my prescriptions on the way home, the effect of that request on me depends on the context. Perhaps you have never abused sharing and helping each other out. In that case, it's no big deal.

But, perhaps you have always abused sharing and helping. Perhaps you have stuck me with running your errands since day one and it's become a big deal in the relationship. I've begged you to take responsibility for some of your own needs.

That would be a whole different context.

If I'm late getting home from work and it only happened once in a while, that's no big deal. But if I have a pattern of being unpredictable, sometimes going out with friends, sometimes going out with other women, sometimes drinking, then it really is a big deal.

This section is about seeing the big picture. Things make sense in the big picture.

1. <u>How we met</u> The beginning of a relationship is a very important event. It has been observed many times in family therapy that relationships usually end for the same reason they started, or for reasons that were present when they started. For example, if I meet you in a bar, we have sex, you get pregnant, and we get married and raise the child, I will probably leave you because of your drinking and sleeping around. If we met at a church we will break up over religious issues or because I complain because you go to church all the time.

    So how did you meet? What were you doing in your life at that time? What was the other person doing? What was the unspoken contract between the two of you about what the relationship meant and what it would consist of?

    <u>Example:</u> "We met at a New Year's Eve party when I was 29 and just divorced, and you were 22 and just out of college. I had just changed career paths for the third time and I was trying to sell real estate. You had just gotten your degree in teaching and started your first teaching job. You were actually making an income but I hadn't started to make any money yet."

2. <u>How long the relationship lasted or has lasted</u>.

    <u>Example:</u> "We have been together nine years. We began living together at your place after we'd only known each other just a few months. You were a little reluctant to let me live with you, but I'd been kicked out of my apartment and had no place else to stay. A year later we got married. Since then we've been separated twice."

3. <u>The track record or history of anger, control, abuse or violence I brought into the relationship.</u> Each of us has seen, experienced or done many things prior to having a relationship. We have had things done to us, and we have done things. If anger, control, abuse or violence became a part of your relationship, it came from somewhere. Where was that?

    Also, if we have had prior relationships, we have a history of doing those things in prior relationships. What did you do? What did it consist of? What is your emotional credit rating?

    <u>Example:</u> "I had been engaged before to a woman I knew in college. I was insecure because her friends thought I wasn't good enough for her, because she was an "A" student with a good future, like her friends, and I was barely making it. I tried to keep her from seeing them because I was jealous. We used to have horrible yelling matches and once I even threatened to kill myself if she didn't see me and only me. I faked an attempt. After that she broke up with me permanently. Between then and the time I met you I only had one girlfriend. I was married her after I'd only known her for a few weeks. We started arguing the day we got married and she left me two months later. She told me I was manipulative and emotionally abusive."

4. <u>Other issues that I brought into the relationship</u>. None of us enter a relationship without baggage. What was yours? Financial issues, personality issues, former relationship issues, self-esteem problems, occupational or educational struggles, things that have happened in your past or other personal or interpersonal problems. What were yours?

   <u>Example</u>: "I have had problems with my self esteem since I was a kid and I have never really made it professionally in any job or career that I've tried. I end up feeling inferior to the people around me and blaming them for my personal problems."

5. <u>Forms of anger, control, abuse, violence I have used in this relationship or toward other people during the relationship</u>. Usually we approach anger, control, abuse and/or violence gradually. Whatever happened which led to your being in the program was preceded by previous abuse, although not necessarily physical. What was it? It also doesn't have to have been toward the current victim. It could have been toward another person or people, such as other people in the family, neighbors, or people at work.

   <u>Example</u>: "All through the relationship I have pressured you to do things that made me feel better or superior. Starting with pressuring you to have sex, tricking you into letting me move in with you, and then bugging you to marry me, I haven't taken your feelings and needs into account much. Just after we got married I wanted to buy a brand new car, now that we had your good credit and steady income. When you wanted to save for a house, which was more reasonable, I withdrew emotionally and later started verbally abusing you. I spent money we couldn't afford out of spite and when you confronted me on it I became physically abusive several times."

6. <u>Issues which have come about in this relationship</u>. These are the events and stressors which have occurred during the relationships. Making or losing money, the births or deaths of children or loved ones. Career changes. Medical issues. What are the things that have charted the course of the relationship?

   <u>Example</u>: "Since we have been together I have tried to control you emotionally and financially and physically. You have given up any hope of really finding any love from me. Meanwhile, I have gotten us hopelessly in debt and you have lost many friends because they are tired of watching what you have had to put up with."

7. <u>How I have exploited your vulnerabilities.</u> Each person has had life experiences or circumstances which make them vulnerable to different things. Some people are afraid of heights. Some people are afraid of rejection. Some people are dependent upon others financially or physically because of handicaps they might have. It's impossible to be with someone who has no vulnerabilities. We all do. The issue is whether or not we take advantage of them. What are the vulnerabilities of the other person which you have taken advantage of?

   <u>Example</u>: "Your father died when you were eleven. You were very close to him and his death was a big trauma for you. You became even closer to your mother after that and you were a really good team. Because of your father's death you have always been trying to find a man you can depend upon, someone to replace him. It also made you afraid of abandonment. I took advantage of that by coming across like an older guy who was really reliable and you could depend upon. You were so afraid of losing me that you put up with lots of crap from me. When one of my friends told you about my faked suicide attempt that completely freaked you out. You were terrified that I might commit suicide and it would be your fault. It made you very afraid to say "no" to me.

8. <u>The history of these issues in the context of my whole life</u>. Shakespeare said "All the world's a stage, and all the men and women merely players. They have their exits and their entrances …" (From *As You Like It* (II,

vii, 139-143)). He was correct. Whatever we are doing at any point in our life is a continuation of the dramas which we started long, long ago. The trouble you are having in this relationship began long before you met and will continue long after. What are those issues? What is that history?

Example: "Somewhere in my childhood there was a fork in the road where I tried to feel good by making other people *make* me feel good, instead of just being a good son, friend, or lover. I have consistently manipulated people all of my life and each time it works less, and each time I lose more. You are just one more example of this. The difference is you loved me and gave me your life and I wasted it."

3. My motive for using anger, control, abuse or violence instead of something appropriate and non-violent

The man in our previous examples could have simply been a good and supportive husband at the party and talked nicely to her about her feelings about the gift and ended up having a good evening. Instead he chose to be selfish, self-centered, and abusive. The question here is, "Why?"

The right way

"I wanted this to be about *me*, not about *you*, and I wanted to use your birthday to draw attention to *me*. I wanted the people at the party to see me as special, so that they would think you were wrong about having second thoughts about me."

The wrong way

"I couldn't take the constant humiliation and I reacted the only way I knew how to defend myself from you."

The reason this is the wrong way is that he still misses the point that he could have handled all these issues in a healthy manner but chose not to, that he had a motive for hurting her feelings. The first one, the right way, is right because it's true; his motive was to draw attention to himself.

4. Why was that wrong?

It's important that we really, really, really know why what we do is wrong. Is it wrong just because it's against the rules? Is it wrong because it gets us in trouble? This is a good place to take the famous "searching moral inventory" to make sure that you know, and can show, why what you did, each thing that you did or left undone, was wrong, and in what ways it was wrong.

The wrong way

"It was wrong to hide money from you because legally it was your money too."

The right way

"I had no right to treat you as though you were born just so I could take things from you. Your possessions, money, rights, needs and feelings are sacred, and not mine to violate. Hiding money from you is the same thing as stealing."

5. The effects it had on the victim

There really aren't any limits to the ways that abuse can affect another person. While the form only mentions four—physical, emotional, financial and "other"—there can be many more which are specific to your situation. Be sure to add whatever effects there are, even if they don't fit in well. Use the "effects" sections of your previous assignments as a guide.

Example:

"Physically; after the fight you were sore for days. The stress and aggravation of it gave you a lot of stress-related disorders that you had to see the doctor for."

"Emotionally: You seem tied up in knots all the time. You are connected to me but you can't trust me. I can see you struggling with contradictory feelings and you are depressed and anxious all the time. I also think that being treated this way for so long has had a bad effect on your self respect."

"Financially; My financial manipulations have set us back financially, both in terms of bad credit and lost money, so badly that it will take years to get our credit up to the point where we can buy a house and start gathering equity and have kids. The cost of court, probation, and treatment adds up to thousands more. It has changed our lifestyle for the worse and forced us to put off having children."

"Other: You have lost friends over this and I even think that the time and trouble and upset have affected your job rating at work."

6. The apology

For an apology to really count it has to be thorough and honest. You have to mean it. Until you can mean it, don't try. Also, never offer an apology and expect it to be accepted or that you will be forgiven. If you do, it's just another skanky form of manipulation, another way to control the other person or force them to forgive you. That's not what this is about. It's none of your business whether or not they forgive you. All that matters is that you apologize well and that you mean it.

To do so you have to be specific about what you did that was wrong and acknowledge that it was wrong.

Wrong way:

"I apologize for any trouble I may or may not have caused by what I have done or left undone."

What the heck does that mean? Nothing! That's not an apology!

Right way:

"I apologize for being a bad guest and companion at your birthday party. I apologize for not helping your Mother out more. I apologize for yelling at you, calling you names, grabbing you, throwing you down, and holding you down. It was the wrong thing to do, I had no right to do it, and I did it out of purely selfish motives."

7. The amends

Amends are what you do to "mend" the damage you did. Look at the "effects" section you wrote above and the "effects" sections of all of your previous assignments. List them out. Now, next to each of them, how you propose to fix or "mend" the damage you did.

As with 12 step programs, you should do your amends "except when to do so would cause more harm." For example if there is a no-contact order, or the other person has moved on and doesn't want to hear from you. In this case, go ahead and write what you would do if you could, or if you were still in the relationship.

The wrong way:

> "I will complete my domestic violence program and become a better person. I will never abuse anyone ever again."

This is the wrong way because it talks about what you are going to do to make yourself a better person, or will not hurt anyone else. This is great. But what about the victim? What are you going to do to repair the damage you did?

The right way:

> "Because I tried to drive away your family and your friends I will contact each one of them personally and explain to them that I was wrong to do what I did and that I support their relationship with you unconditionally. And from now on, any time and every time any friend or family wants to talk to you or do something with you I won't interfere and I will do everything I can to make them comfortable."

This is the right way because it actually repairs the damage you have done.

As with all the assignments in the INVENTORY section you are required to get a signature from a witness to make your commitment to these changes a meaningful part of your life, and it needs to be a different witness than in the prior exercises.

ASSIGNMENT TWENTY FIVE
THE RESPONSIBILITY LETTER

"Dear...." _____

1. What I did to you in the immediate event _____

2. The context in which it occurred _____

   How we met _____

   How long the relationship was _____

   The track record or history of anger, control, abuse, or violence I brought into the relationship _____

   Other issues that I brought into the relationship _____

   Forms of anger, control, abuse, and/or violence I have used in this relationship or toward other people during the relationship. _____

   Issues which have come about in this relationship _____

   How I have exploited your vulnerabilities. _____

   The history of these issues in the context of my whole life. _____

3. My Motive for doing it _____

4. Why that was wrong _____

5. The effects it had on you or other victims _____

   Physically _____

   Emotionally _____

   Financially _____

   Other ways _____

6. My apology _____

7. My amends _____

I _____ am hereby committing to taking responsibility for my actions, to making my amends, and to living as a non-controlling, non-abusive, non-violent person.

_____ ___/___/___ _____ ___/___/___
(My name)   (Witnessed by)

LESSON TWENTY SIX:

THE EMPATHY LETTER

Could you imagine hitting yourself in the face? It would be difficult because you know it would hurt. But we can hit someone else in the face. Unless, that is, we were aware of how it felt to them. If we could genuinely feel their pain. Then it would be as difficult to hurt them as it would be to cause the same pain to ourselves.

That is what empathy is. Empathy is the ability to feel the pain and suffering, the joys and sorrows, the tragedies and triumphs of another person.

If we could genuinely see ourselves as others see us, if we could genuinely understand the impact of what we are saying and doing, we could never control or abuse a loved one. Much less be violent. It would be unthinkable.

The empathy letter is a test to see if you can understand what the other person felt and feels. Remember, if you truly understand and can feel the feelings of the other person, you can't control or abuse them, any more than you could grub your eye out of it's socket with a stick.

The EMPATHY LETTER is like a Responsibility Letter, but in reverse. It's from the other person's perspective, as if they were writing a letter to you, in their words. And not what they would say if they were being polite.

"Dear...."
1. "What you did to me in the immediate situation."
2. "The context in which it occurred."

   a. How we met
   b. How long the relationship was
   c. Your personal history which you brought into this relationship.
   d. The track record or history of anger, control, abuse, or violence you brought into the relationship to the best of my knowledge
   e. Other issues that you brought into the relationship
   f. Forms of anger, control, abuse, and/or violence you have used in this relationship or toward me or other people during the relationship.
   g. Issues which have come about in this relationship
   h. How you have exploited my vulnerabilities.
   i. Where this abuse fits into the story of my life and my prior experiences.

3. "Why what you did to me was wrong"

4. "The effects it had on me"

    a. Physically
    b. Emotionally
    c. Financially
    d. Other ways
5. "The apology I expect."
6. "The amends I expect."

Example

1. What you did to me in the immediate event and how it felt at the time

"Dear Steve. I knew there was going to be trouble the day before my birthday. You appeared so bitter and resentful and made lots of comments about how you would have done the birthday different if my family hadn't interfered. I kept offering to talk about it but you'd smile this weird smile and just say that nothing was wrong and that you'd been looking forward to my birthday all year.

When we went to my Mother's house you were outright nasty. I couldn't say or do anything right. Once we got there you sat back by yourself. You didn't talk to anyone or do anything or even help out until my Mom asked you directly. Even then you appeared like you were ready to pop.

I loved the ring and I always will, but I was so afraid of saying or doing anything wrong that I just kissed you and told you I loved you and went on with the other gifts.

You told me we had to leave early because the sitter had to get home. I was really surprised by that. After all, it was my birthday. But I said goodbye to the guests and we went home. As soon as the car was out of sight of the house you ripped into me with all your hate and resentment. You told me I was a bad wife and that I was ungrateful for the gift. There was nothing I could say that would stop you. I couldn't help but cry, and that just made you madder.

You continued into the house with your yelling and cursing. The sitter saw and heard this. After you paid her and she left you continued your yelling. I begged you to stop. I was afraid you'd wake up the kids. You grabbed me and threw me down on the sofa and got your face in my face and screamed at me. I struggled and got up and you grabbed me and threw me on the ground. The kids started to cry in their bedrooms so I called the police while you left the room. I was so ashamed. But I didn't know what else to do."

2 The context in which it occurred

 1. How we met

    "We met at a New Year's Eve party at the house of a mutual friend. You were just divorced and so cute and so sad that I couldn't help but feel sorry for you and want to comfort you. One thing led to another and we moved from me holding you and comforting you to you touching me sexually and wanting to have sex. I'd only known you a half hour but you begged and insisted and said you needed this and eventually I gave in. I felt really weird about it."

 2. How long the relationship was

    "We've been together seven years. You wanted to move in right away, right after we met, you just showed up at my door and said you'd been kicked out of your apartment and had no place else to go. I really had no choice, so I gave in. Then you wanted to get married right away. As soon as we got married I learned how in debt you were and you told me that you had changed your mind, you didn't want to have children, that we couldn't afford to have children. I felt tricked and cheated."

3. <u>Your personal history which you brought into this relationship.</u>

    "I had no way of knowing the personal and professional problems you brought into the relationship. You had an unstable job, a lot of financial problems, and no real history of having healthy relationships."

4. <u>The track record or history of anger, control, abuse, or violence you brought into the relationship to the best of my knowledge</u>

    "I found out later that you had manipulated, tricked, and emotionally abused both of the previous women you'd been with. When I learned this I began doubting my judgment and never again felt safe with anything you ever said or did."

5. <u>Other issues that you brought into the relationship</u>

    "I felt overwhelmed by all the personal and professional problems you brought with you. If it wasn't one thing, it was something else. It was almost like another painful discovery every few months the whole time I've known you."

6. <u>Forms of anger, control, abuse, and/or violence you have used in this relationship or toward me or other people during the relationship.</u>

    "You have pressured me into a relationship I wasn't ready for. You lied to me about your history and what you would be able to do. You have tried to isolate me from friends and family, you have taken my money, you have verbally abused me, you have endangered my job, you assaulted me, and you did it in front of the kids.

7. <u>Issues which have come about in this relationship</u>

    "Since we have been married you have lost several jobs, driven off several of my friends. You have become very insecure and an emotional liability."

8. <u>How you have exploited my vulnerabilities.</u>

    "When we first met you knew that my father had died when I was eleven and that my mother and I survived by relying on each other. You knew how much I wanted to be married just once and to not get divorced or be abandoned, not have to face the fact that I had married a fake. Once I learned about your suicide attempts I was terrified of what you might do if I didn't go along with everything you wanted."

9. <u>Where this abuse fits into the story of my life and my prior experiences.</u>

    "My whole life I've wanted to be married and have a family. Everything was supposed to lead up to this point. Now all my plans have had to change. This isn't what I wanted, what I dreamed about and worked for. This is exactly what I didn't want for my life. I don't want to raise my children in an abusive home but I don't want to have to put them through what I lived through as a child."

<u>3. Why what you did was wrong</u>

"You had no right to spoil my birthday, my life, or to ruin the happiness of my children. Our rights and feelings and needs are valid, just like yours are."

<u>4. The effects it had on me</u>
- e. Physically "I was bruised and sore for days. I couldn't sleep well and was so upset that I couldn't eat or work."
- f. Emotionally "I cried for days, I'm always nervous now, and I have no respect for you or for myself for putting up with it. I don't' feel right in my own skin. Sometimes my life feels so 'wrong' that it doesn't seem real, it doesn't seem like it could be *my* life."
- g. Financially "I have missed several promotions because I was spending all my time and energy trying to appease you and not paying attention to my job. It will take years to recreate my credit ratings, if ever. You cost us the cost of living apart while you had the no contact order, and the legal and counseling costs."
- h. Other ways "I don't know if you could ever repair the damage you did to my relationships with my friends and families. I can never feel clean or innocent ever again."

<u>5. The apology I expect</u> "I expect you to apologize to me, to the children and to my family and friends, without making excuses."

<u>6. The amends I expect</u> "I expect you to apologize to the people you have manipulated and lied to, to tell the truth, to get an extra job or work overtime or whatever you have to do until you have paid the family back for what you have taken away, and repaired our credit history, and I want you to make our house and our home a safe, nurturing place where we never have to worry again about what you'll do next."

For this final exercise in your program, remember to get a signature for the fifth and final witness to whom you are making this commitment to change.

ASSIGNMENT TWENTY SIX
THE EMPATHY LETTER

"Dear...." _____

1. What you did to me in the immediate event and how it felt at the time

2. The context in which it occurred

   a) How we met _____

   b) How long the relationship was _____

   c) Your personal history which you brought into this relationship. _____

   d) The track record or history of anger, control, abuse, or violence you brought into the relationship to the best of my knowledge _____

   e) Other issues that you brought into the relationship _____

   f) Forms of anger, control, abuse, and/or violence you have used in this relationship or toward me or other people during the relationship. _____

   g) Issues which have come about in this relationship _____

   h) My vulnerabilities which you have taken advantage of and which make the things that you have done to me or left undone that much more painful.

   i) Where this abuse fits into the story of my life and my prior experiences.

3. Why what you did was wrong

4. The effects it had on me
   a) Physically _____

   b) Emotionally _____

   c) Financially _____

   d) Other ways _____

5. The apology I expect

6. The amends I expect

I _____ am hereby committing to taking responsibility for my actions, to making my amends, and to living as a non-controlling, non-abusive, non-violent person.

_____ ___/___/___   _____ ___/___/___
     (My name)   (Witnessed by)

Thank you very much for the chance to work together for the last twenty-six weeks. You have worked hard to get to this point and shared this experience with the other men in your group.

This is just the beginning. The next step is six months of individual therapy to address the shortcomings, inadequacies, and issues which you have identified in the last six months. At the end of that six month period, if you have met all the criteria set forth by law and in your contract with the program, you can leave the program, or continue on a voluntary basis.

Changing a behavior, a way of thinking or relating, which is so clearly supported by our media, our government, our heroes and leaders, is not easy. We live in an abusive, controlling, and even violent world. It's hard to stay sane in an insane situation, it's hard to stay sober in a bar, it's hard to stay celibate in a brothel.

And it's hard to be non-controlling, non-abusive, and non-violent in our society today. It's a lifetime commitment to taking the high road even when you can get away with being sloppy. You are welcome back at any time if things get hard or if you find yourself slipping.

Thanks again for all you've done, and for all that you may continue to become in the future!

978-0-595-47848-4
0-595-47848-4